# KICKING

## KARMA'S ASS

Unbelievable Stories of Strength, Resilience, and Perseverance, All Told with a Twist of Humor

## Pat Miller

This work depicts actual events in the life of the author as truthfully as recollection permits. While all persons within are actual individuals, names and identifying characteristics have been changed to respect their privacy.

**Dedicated to my best friend, high school sweetheart and late husband, Ray Miller.**

Ray was a simple, blue collar man who provided a good life for me and my two sons with his sweat and hard work. We were friends, business partners and lovers. He was the calm when I was the storm.

The pain he endured from his bladder cancer was unfathomable, especially when it metastasized to his sciatic nerve, yet, he never complained. He was selfless, always worried about me and the boys in a time of extreme suffering.

Ray prepared me for life without him in so many ways that I never realized until after his passing. His death allowed me to become the woman I was destined to be. He walks with me every day, and sends me lots of feathers and coins as a reminder he is now my angel.

Thank you for watching  over me babe.  Until we meet again...rest in peace my love 🖤🕊️

# Contents

# Foreword

My name is Ingrid Baird and Lord knows I've experienced many trials and tribulations to get where I am today. At the release of this book, I am currently a Lieutenant in a police department in New Jersey, and a Crisis Negotiator Team Leader on our Regional Swat team. I hold a Master's Degree in Public Administration and am a single mother of three.

When Pat told me she was writing a book and asked if I would write the Foreword, I was beside myself and honored. I think it's important to share stories that empower women, to give hope to those who just can't seem to see the silver lining in every cloud. I live my life believing everything happens for a reason. My meeting Patricia Miller was nothing short of that. Girl Power is a thing. You'd be surprised to know how many of us are really bad asses and take no shit. Pat is one tough mama.

Have you ever met someone and thought, "Oh my God, they were heaven sent"? Well, that's how I felt when I first met Pat and her husband Ray. Our meeting was not coincidence, it was fate. In mid 2014, I was in the process of rebuilding my house thanks to Hurricane Sandy. I was only four blocks from the beach, and like so many others, lost everything.  I was a single mother of three working diligently to gather any information I could to make it a smooth transition for my family.  The surrounding areas held meetings designed to align families with connections to services they may need to move forward in rebuilding their lives.  I came upon a company that offered module homes as a solution to get displaced families back into their homes quickly.  Many months had passed since we lost our home and it sounded perfect for us.

After many meetings and signing of documents, I hired the company. There was a significant amount of red tape I had to get through to apply and be approved for federal monies. So when I handed over a seventy-six thousand dollar check to start my new home, I made it very clear that everything had better be on the up and up because we were dealing with federal money. I also added to it, making the grand total upwards of a hundred grand. The man assured me it was all fine.

But that all changed when, several weeks later, I received a phone call from an unknown number.  I reluctantly answered it; I never pick up calls from unknown numbers. On the other end, I hear a female's voice, "Hi my name is Patricia Miller. I'm the owner of Blue Diamond, the company subcontracted to build your home. I'm in possession of all your original documents. I wanted to let you know that I'm not sure what the deal is, but I am not comfortable proceeding with any business agreements with the company you hired. With that said, I would not feel right if I did not deliver your documents back to you personally. After you get your original documents back you can decide what you would like to do, mainly because if I give them back to this man I feel he will have the ability to hold you hostage and then your options will be limited." During this conversation Pat shared her concerns with me, the biggest one being that this company did not hold the proper connections, the proper licenses nor the proper insurance to take on such a project. She not only brought me my documents, she compiled a list of things I should ask the company. I never would have known what to ask to make sure they were able to handle my project. His answers to all my questions were a big fat NO. Needless to say, they were fired and I hired Pat and Ray. That was how our beautiful relationship bloomed. I loved her strong, no nonsense business woman style. She got shit done. Ray was the man that put the plan together and delivered a one-of-a-kind home to a feisty Puerto Rican and her kids. Now there is something you should know about this tough lady: Patricia Miller is a kind giving person, with a side of, *I'll come for your soul if you dare try me.* I think we share this quality and why we hold the relationship we have until this day. What I love the most about our friendship is no hidden agendas. Back then, she saved me from more problems than I can imagine. After I was back in my brand new home my life was full of happiness, joy and hope. This did not hold true for Pat's life.

This book will take you through Pat's journey of overcoming obstacles that would be best categorized as climbing Mount Everest, barefoot. No matter what life threw her way she made a conscious decision to win. Pat overcomes chaos with a smile and definitely with a good pair of boots because no one knows how to kick karma's ass like she does.

My family and I will forever be indebted to her and for this reason I've always called her my Angel.

# *Introduction*

Growing up with a strict Italian father and a loving Irish mother, I was taught subservience as a way of life. The man was the breadwinner and provider, while the woman was the heart of the home, tending to the children and household chores. I often say children learn what they live. Those old school teachings were tattooed into my brain. So much so, I carried them straight into my own marriage. Although my strong personality didn't allow for the level of subservience my mother demonstrated, it was a deeply ingrained personality trait. Like my mother before me, my husband took center stage, by design.

I was his shadow in the distance, the unknown necessary, diligently working behind the scenes. I often told my husband, "Hey, just remember babe, behind every successful man is a strong woman supporting him." He would chuckle, knowing that I teed him up for success.

You might not think a subservient woman would be grateful for her role in the background, but I was, and I am. What is most remarkable now is that since his death, our roles are reversed. He is behind the scenes supporting me like I once supported him. My husband's death prompted an incredible transformation in my life.

Not in a million years did I ever imagine having to rebuild the future without my crutch and support system in place. Admittedly, I was never a shrinking violet, but taking center stage was the scariest thing I've ever had to do alone. As the saying goes, "You don't get less afraid, you get more bold."

My kids tell me, "Ma, stop talking to people like they owe you two million dollars! You are *very* intimidating." I don't know when to turn it off. As the youngest of seven, being loud was a survival skill; being assertive meant getting fed, usually. I wish I was kidding, but growing up dirt-poor ain't no joke.

I'm Patricia Miller. Friends and associates call me Pat; to family, I'm Tish, Trish or Patty. As the sole owner of Blue Diamond Construction, my guys call me "Lady boss." For 30-plus years, I have been working in the commercial metal framing business in New Jersey. My company frames large commercial buildings the average person uses everyday.

As a woman in a man's world, I need to come across with a bit of an edge. Early childhood 'training' prepared me for real life, where I would have to fight to keep what was mine. In business, the men I work with try to steal my money. This isn't chump change - we're talking millions of dollars. When asked what I do for a living, I smile and say, "I sling steel and keep mens' hands outta my pockets, and you?"

If I don't hold my own in a meeting, or on the jobsite running 40 men, they treat me as if I'm there to deliver payroll. I'll never forget the first meeting held for a big job. All the engineers, architects, owner's reps, foremen for all the companies; everybody was there. Of the 21 people attending, I was the only woman.

The electrician started talking down to me like I was some dumb blonde. He was a condescending jerk who dug his own hole, which didn't take long at all. "You're not doing this, you're not doing that, and you are not putting drywall up on the fifth floor. I'll *allow you* to do 20 boards," he said.

With that, the room fell stone-cold silent.

All of a sudden, the guys who knew me pushed their chairs back away from the table, crossed their arms over their chests and waited; all eyes were on me.

I admit, I wasn't very nice to him, but this is what can happen in my line of work. If you don't stand your ground, you lose it; there are thousands of people vying for space on a job. So I turned to him and said, "Oh, really? You're not gonna *allow* me? I think you've got the wrong fucking girl, OK? You sit there and keep your fucking mouth shut. You are gonna put your wires through the fucking studs that *I put* where this building needs to be laid out. Remember that: I do the work, *you follow me.*"

You could have heard a pin drop. He was catching flies with his mouth hanging open so long, I swear. Everybody burst out laughing except him, of course. A few days later, his name was nothing but a funny story to tell: he got transferred off the job. *Some dumb blonde, huh?* Think again, pal. I had nothing to do with his transfer, by the way. Chock it up to karma, man.

Since I was a kid, I've had a big mouth. Even so, as a woman on the job, I don't want to be labeled "the bitch," the one who screams "lawsuit" over cat calls, or 'that woman' who gets emotional once a month. I've had to learn to walk the fine line between being loud and being heard.

Working sixty, eighty-plus hour weeks for years, my husband, Ray, a metal framing carpenter, built half of New Jersey. What started with a hundred bucks in flyers and business cards became a multi-million-dollar home-based

18

business. I learned the basics with degrees in accounting and business. From there, it was sweat equity. You don't need three letters behind your name to make it in this world. All you need is focus, resilience and perseverance to handle the crap that comes your way, so it doesn't get *in* your way.

It helps to have a sense of humor, too.

Take the day our job's plumber stumbled upon the Superintendent's truck. He was going to knock on the window, but found the man stroking-off to cat porn. You can't unsee a thing like that. It's crazy how all the guys knew about it, but not one of them ever said a word.

I was glad the plumber told me. As much as we needed that job, I had to say *something*. I never thought I would see a G.C. (General Contractor) blush, but ours did. Then he got nervous; twitchy, almost. *Would it have landed better if a guy said something, first?* I wondered. As if the worst part of the story is *me* being the one who said something, right? Another woman might have pressed charges - and won. These days, an exposed penis is considered a weapon. Imagine the headline: *Construction Super Fired for Possession of a Loaded Weapon.* Neither of them would have ever recovered. Fortunately, it didn't go that way…it went even better.

Carl's obsession with cat porn could have been left at home, but nooo, he brought it to work. Like, *How bad is it, buddy, that you have to jack-off to cat porn at 6AM in your SUV?* Maybe new videos had just been uploaded and he couldn't contain his excitement? Ahem.

*So, you really love cats, do ya? Let's see how much, Carl.* I put stuffed animal cats in the johns, hung them on his golf cart, and glued them to his work box. Watching him take a swing at the stuffed cat hanging from his rearview mirror was priceless. I'm pretty sure the BDSM kitty pissed him off the most: I cut eye holes in black electrical tape and wrapped it around the cat's head like a mask. A sign, "Beat me, I like it!" was taped to the cat's chest.

Every prank was in plain sight - and within earshot.

Hell, I even bought a case of Friskies Cat Buffet and left open cans on his truck hood, jobsite trailer stairs and tool bucket. Imagine reaching in for a screw gun and getting a finger full of Friskies Pate Ocean Whitefish, instead. For all we know he liked it. Or licked it.

For months we heard, "Fuck! Fuck! FUUUUUCK!! Goddamnit, Pat!" The only thing funnier was us busting a gut, *again*, at his expense.

In life, we seldom get the chance to watch someone squirm like Carl, but he had it coming. In fact, what I did was nothing compared to what he truly deserved. He intentionally screwed with my life and tried to crush my business. What a guy. Here's the plot twist: Carl's lying, manipulative, cold-hearted actions actually paved the way for my healing. I just didn't see it that way for quite some time. Perspective changes everything.

# It all started here...

In 2013, my oldest brother died. In 2014, Mom passed away. In 2015, dad died of a broken-heart. Losing his wife of 64 years was too much. All of this was too much.

I prayed to St. Jude, the patron saint of difficult cases. Every day, I prayed so hard for their comfort, for a miracle recovery, and for time. *'Please, just a little more time? This came on so suddenly.'* I prayed so much the saints must have been like, "Oh, it's *her* again."

No angels came. No signs from heaven came, assuring me it was going to be OK. No proof that miracles happen at all. No, instead, on November 11, 2014, Ray, my husband of 30 years, was diagnosed with cancer.

One unsuccessful cancer trial later, over a *million dollars of savings spent and $250,000* in the hole with high interest loans, and exactly two years to the day, on November 11, 2016, my high school sweetheart passed away.

One day after his funeral, I put my boots on and headed back to the job site. If I didn't, the contract, the income we, now I, so desperately needed, would have died, too. How much loss can one person take?

**You never know how strong you are until being strong is your only option.**

Life's most unlikely, horrific, traumatic events can leave you in a heap on the ground, or have you soul-searching to find meaning beyond the chaos. Will you build your own set of wings and Phoenix your way out of it, or wallow in the woes of what happened?

You can let negative experiences ruin you, or not. Sometimes you crash. It hurts, but you can get back up again if you want to. You have to really want to, though. And sometimes, even then, it doesn't work out the way you wanted it to. Sometimes, it works out even better.

# One

Liz grabbed the bottle of wine and stumbled a bit, overpouring with a smile. It was 'Kitchen Karaoke' night at my house: time to drink too much, dance our asses off and solve the world's problems. My being single appeared to be one of Liz's biggest problems.

"Patty, Ray told you to go find somebody you can talk to, have coffee with, talk to about work. You know, somebody you can travel with like you guys were going to do? He wanted you to have a life." I nodded. He knew he was dying. And he knew I didn't like to be alone. Ray's insistence that I move on was very selfless.

My brother, on the other hand, didn't get to have that conversation with his wife. He said, "You and Ray got to talk about it, but she died in my arms in a matter of days. I didn't get to hear her say 'it's OK to find someone else'."

Life throws curve balls. For others, it's a wrecking ball. I guess my brother decided to sit in the rubble. "I just can't, Patty." And so it is, to this day.

I thought back to one of my mother's favorite expressions, "Life is for the living. If you don't have a life, you're not living."

"You helped Ray crossover, Patty. It's time for you to move on, too." Liz was right. Two years before, I sat at his bedside for the final time. "It's ok to go, Ray. Go, go, *go* to the light!" In the same vein, he wanted me to move on, too.

But what did I know about dating? I was with the same man since high school.

"Come on girl, it's time to kick up those high heels again! WuHOOO!" Liz was the type of friend who would take a bullet for you. I trusted her and knew she meant well. Still, she wasn't the one dating for the first time. Being plunged into the dating scene was like jumping in the ocean in January.

I turned the music up louder if only to buy myself some time to think. *Was it really time? Shouldn't I wait a little longer? What's the right amount of time to wait for a widow, anyway? How do you know you're ready? What do I say to strangers? 'Hi, I'm Patty. I lost my brother, mother, father, husband and over a million dollars in life savings in a three year period. But hey, I'm over it now. What was your name, again?'*

She shouted at me over the music, "You hate being alone in this big-ass house *and you know it!*"

I forced a smile. That's what Kitchen Karaoke was for: two good friends, wine, music, belting out songs like rock stars. Nothing serious. Why change it? I'm sure she expected me to say, 'No, not yet,' like I had a million times before.

"OK!" I shouted back, "How?? Where do we start?"

You'd have thought she won a trip to Hawaii. I could hardly contain her excitement. Out came the cell phones. I think her hands were shaking more than mine. This was a huge step.

"Oh! Yes!! Finallllly! Let's get you on a dating site!"

*Wait, what?*

Blame it on the wine, or the Divine, I agreed to try dating online. I half-wondered if Ray was watching us, but kept those thoughts to myself. No sense being a buzzkill. See? I have a filter, sometimes.

"I'll write a raving profile about you. You are amazing, girl!" Liz stepped back and made a frame with her hands like I was somethin' special. "Don't let all of this go to waste, girl! You have too much to offer, I swear!"

Then the inevitable, the dreaded, "Let's take some pictures!" I'd rather stick pins in both eyes. But the wine was talkin' and her timing was perfect. *Plenty of Fish*, it was.

Guys, cast your rods. Oh wait, that didn't come out right at all…

The next day she called to ask how it was going.

I said, "Apparently, I'm, uh, well, I'm sexy?"

She was like, "Duh, I told you!!"

When you're married that many years, "Hey, sexy" wasn't part of the program anymore. It's still weird to hear the words. The men at work wouldn't dare treat me 'that way' but men online were different. They didn't mind lettin' it all hang out, literally. It was a bit much.

Several hundred responses came in from every kind of man I didn't want. I prefer men with teeth, who aren't wearing a stained Black Sabbath T-shirt with long hair and even longer beards. I wondered what we might do for fun, like, maybe braid each other's hair? It wasn't for me, that's all I knew. Underwhelmed, we deleted my profile. There had to be better fish in the sea.

"Bumble. That's what my co-workers said we should do, Patty." It was another Karaoke Kitchen night. Bumble sounded better than Fish. Classier guys, but still 'meat market' vibes. At least "Joe" was well-groomed with slicked-back jet black hair and a really nice smile. So many of the guys don't even smile in their photos. Maybe there's a reason, like, they don't have pearly whites or something? Guys, women go for good teeth, so flash 'em if you got 'em.

Joe said he was the executive chef and owner of a restaurant. I figured it'd be nice to have someone cook me a meal for once. We chatted, had similar interests, and agreed to meet for a drink at a restaurant I know very well.

If a picture is worth a thousand words, Joe's picture had about 20 years' worth of catching up to do. He resembled himself, sort of. I was willing to look past the misrepresentation. Conversation, chemistry and connection is what mattered the most to me. But first, some small talk, like "Hey, Joe, what's the name of your restaurant?"

He looked around the restaurant, as if searching the air for an answer. "Yeah, well, I uh just bought some pots and pans. I'm gonna go into catering," he said. "You know, I got the equipment. I'll get the restaurant next."

"Yah, sure, Joe. That's like me saying I don't build commercial buildings, yet, but I have all the tools to do it, so that makes me a commercial builder."

Don't try to play me, man. Not a good start. Dang it. He was cute, too.

I was okay with him telling me how beautiful I was, but when he said he liked my small feet more than a few times,

I mentally buckled-up. This guy was a trip and I was along for the ride.

"Would you like a drink? I'll go get us somethin'." I watched him and his tired Italian loafers stride over to the bar. His jeans fit nice. I wondered why he had an outline on the back pocket where his wallet was, though. I mean, it takes a long time for that to happen to a pair of jeans, right? Still, his confidence was sexy. Overriding the few red flags I thought, *What the heck? Everybody deserves a chance.*

"I will have a glass of champagne, thanks, Joe." He was gone so long I thought he was out back stomping grapes in his loafers, I swear.

He finally came back, empty-handed. In that thick Staten Island accent of his, said, "The bahr tendas busy." I knew better. I knew the bartender, too. He was an efficient sorta guy.

"Ohhh, OK, Joe." Trying to play me again, huh? Hmmm.

I let it slide. More small talk. It was going well until I said, "Listen, I'm going to get myself a drink."

"No, no, no, let me go get it." He motioned for me to sit back down and wait. "I'll be right back, Patty."

This time, I watched him the whole way. Although he walked around to the far side, I could see his worn-out shoes through the gap in the bar. He just stood there for like five minutes, then came back and said, "The bahr tenda's still busy." And I'm still thirsty, thanks.

Uh-huh. I debated on how serious of a verbal assault weapon I wanted to be. *"Ma! You got no filter!"* ran through my head. Sometimes, that's not a bad thing, son. I let loose. "You're fucking broke aren't you, Joe?"

Well, that was like opening up the floodgates of the Hoover dam. He went off on a tangent saying, "Those fucking feds! They took everything I own: all my debit cards, all my credit cards and my bank accounts, too. I have to start my life over after 10 years. Years ago, I'd have nice fancy cars to take out beautiful women like you, and now I gotta get dropped off on a date, *by my son,* with no fuckin' money."

I was like wha wha wha *what*? "What the fuck did you do to land yourself in federal prison for 10 years?"

He instantly turned into a Joe Pesci mobster character, turning his head to the side, looking up at the ceiling and saying, "I didn't do nuttin'."

I laughed and said, "Come on, Joe, the feds don't get it wrong when you sit in prison for 10 years."

A normal woman would have run by now. But I found it intriguing so I pushed myself away from the cocktail table, folded my arms and said, "You know, Joe, I'm gonna stick around to hear this one. Now, *seriously,* what the fuck did you do to spend 10 years in federal prison?"

"OK…OK…somethin' blew up." He glanced at me, then back up at the ceiling. "But I didn't do it. I just drove the caaar, I swear!" I laughed even harder.

I looked at him, he looked back at me, and then he says in his heavy Staten Island accent, "So you wan' me to call ya an Uber now or wha'?"

"No, Joe I have my own car. It's more like, do you want me to call an Uber for you?"

"I like you, you're funny…but no, I'll call my son." We both laughed our asses off.

In parting I said, "Hey, Joe, if the restaurant business doesn't pan out you can always be an Uber driver. That's what landed you 10 years in federal prison, *driving,* right?"

"Oh, you're fucking hysterical."

So are you, Joe. I'm *still* laughing.

P.S. Pesci Joe is back in prison, but he didn't do nuttin'.

My sons would be proud their mother has a filter. Well, maybe it's more of a finely-crafted skill in telling white lies than it is a filter. I'm not so sure they'd be proud of that bit, but it's a start. And there is a very good reason for it.

Most every message started out with 'I can't believe someone as sexy as you is single.' How do you respond to that? *Why, yes I am, and, yes I am. Let me see your teeth.*

"So, Beautiful, what do you do for a living?" The inevitable small talk question. I used to tell the truth, but now I just say, "I'm self-employed."

"Oh, what are you, a hair dressa?" I don't know why that's the go-to guess. Maybe it's my blonde hair and hot pink fingernails?

I twirl my hair and say "Yeaaah, I'm a hair dressa." I met a lot of "My Cousin Vinny" types. I can't tell them I build large commercial buildings. They either get intimidated, call me a liar, or hit me up for a job. "Hey, uh, Pat, I got skills. You hirin'? Can you get me on a job?"

I want to say, "Listen, buddy, if I wanted to date a coworker I would have done that already. And no, I can't find you a spot on a job somewhere else, either." These guys ought to be meeting with a head hunta not a hair dressa.

There are little white lies to spare feelings. Those get a pass. It's the big lies, and the liars who tell them, that have got to go. Before you know it, their hands are in your pockets to take *whatever* you have: a heart, hope or hundo's, it doesn't matter. At least, not to them, it doesn't.

For once I'd like to meet a man who is strong, well-to-do, a sharp dresser, a smart business man – and one who appreciates an old school wife. That's how I was raised, you know? I always served Ray his dinner. It drove our sons nuts. "What's the problem? That's what my mother did. Your father worked all day so I'm making up his plate. Big deal." I saw that as loving, not sexist.

But now, I have this fantasy life in mind, where my biggest concern is going to the mall to find a pair of shoes that match my bag.

Yeah, right.

That would last about five minutes and I'd be in the purse manufacturing business, telling my man to cook his own dinner. Maybe. It's hard to change your own tune. I happen to like being a caregiver. It's just that, well, sometimes, I want to give, and all they want is to take.

The red Ferrari caught my attention. *What do we have here?* Fast cars are a hobby of mine. The men who drive them make for interesting conversation.

"Hi, my name's Richard, but please call me Rick."

I was looking for that special man; the one Ray promised to send my way. Was this him? Rick seemed to have his act together. During our first date he asked me, "Tell me something I don't know about you, yet."

I might have said, *I like watching kitchen gadget infomercials at 3am.* At least it would have left the door open for banter about air fryers. But no, instead, no-filter me said, "I'm going to be your deathbed regret." Whoa. Where did that come from? Somehow, it felt true, or that it was going to be true.

Rick was oddly familiar to me, like we knew each other before and were just picking up where we left off. I wanted to go with *that* feeling, and believe good luck had finally come my way. Truth was, something in me knew *this isn't going to fucking work out.* Why else would I have blurted-out 'deathbed regret' on Day 1? Weird. But I saw potential and dug in with both high heels.

I helped this man more times than fingers on both hands. He would do something really offensive, stupid or insulting, and I would give him another chance. You gotta look past the bad behavior, hang onto potential, and see greater for others, right? That's what fixers do.

Liz said, "Pat, what are you doing?? You're smarter than this! You deserve better than him! You give and he takes. You're the one who does nice things and he gives back evil deeds. What IS it with this guy?" Liz heard all the stories of disappointment Rick shoveled my way.

I kept giving him chances, over and over again. He would apologize, change for a little while, then pull another wicked stunt. By this time, he was deep into my world in every way. He was my vested interest, so, I kept holding onto tiny improvements as signs of progress.

It was embarrassing, even to me. "I don't know, Liz. I don't get it either. I've cut people out of my life for far less than this guy's done to me. It's like I can't stop. I just don't understand why I feel compelled to help him!"

He clearly needed my help: with a job, with a solid girlfriend, with a direction in life. The perfect case for a fixer, I was showing him how to build the good life he said he wanted to offer me. As my first relationship since Ray passed away, my heart was open and full of hope.

My sons didn't like him. In fact, nobody did. Still, they gave me the space to figure it out on my own, and I give them heaps of credit for letting Mom make her own mistakes.

But when an email arrived from a woman in Connecticut, all hell broke loose. Rick was *her* boyfriend. Hers and apparently that of several other women in three other states. Now I know why they make those movies: my life became a "Lifetime Movie of the Week," too. I imagined a call like this:

"Hello, is this Ms. Miller?"

*Yes.*

"This is the Lifetime Network. We've been doing some digging around and it seems you've been keeping the company of one shifty son-of-a-bitch. We think it would make a good movie of the week, don't you?"

*If only that POS were worth the cost of the film, sir. But yeah, he pulled-off quite the stunt. Still is, in fact. It's a story that needs to be told because it isn't just happening on TV.*

I could imagine what might be said next.

"Uhm, ma'am, is there a reason why you continued to see him after you first noticed he was a piece of shit?"

*Look, I'm guilty of one thing: trying to polish a turd. I'm chocking it up to being a fixer, to fate, and one helluva fuck-up. Take that how you want...*

When I thought he had his act together, I had no idea it was *all* an act. I fell for a fake, a forgery of a person who was nothing even close to the invented stories of his past, or present. That womanizing con man hustled those other women out of thousands of dollars, property, and even a master's degree. Huh? A master's degree? Yes, a story in itself.

My biggest loss was time. I lost years on empty promises and head games. Recovering from the shock was hard enough. My heart was shattered. After all I'd been through, to have this jerk show up was like, *WHY, God? Why would you send me such an asshole? What did I do to deserve this?*

The final nail was a text from Rick. It followed an 'I love you' text. Yep, he was letting me know how excited he was about being engaged. He found someone new to soak life was coming up roses. That self-professed, single-forever, "don't believe in marriage" son-of-a-bitch was getting *married?* What the hell??

"Trish, I will always love you and I want to remain friends," he wrote. "If you ever need anything please don't hesitate to call me, I will be there in a flash."

"Are you fucking kidding me, Rick?!"

He replied, "What's the matter? Aren't you happy for me?"

Thrilled. Words escape me. *May you have the life you deserve.*

*I'm smarter than this.* At least, that's what I thought. Surely something else was at-play here? If everything happens for a reason, then what was the reason for this shit? How could it possibly serve to have my kindness taken for weakness?

On top of it all, I beat myself up pretty hard for months afterward. We all do it. Just keep in mind that trying to mend a broken heart when you're busy boxing your own ears doesn't help the hurt stop hurting.

Could this have been avoided, or was it fated to occur? Was there some D&M, (Deep and Meaningful) reason for it? Is that why I stuck it out longer than I would have normally? Was it my karma? Was it his? Was this payback? Was my lesson learned? If so, what the hell was it?

At the time, there seemed to be no good explanation. God let me down, and my patron saint for hopeless cases pulled another no-show.

Ironically, Richard catalyzed spiritual growth in ways I never anticipated. So, thanks, *Dick*. That is your name, right?

# Two

After Ray died, I decided to start treating myself to facials and beauty treatments at Jacquelyn's aesthetics salon. People called us "Bonnie & Clyde," the hellraisers, but we knew each other as 'Jax and Patsy.' A strong business woman with a huge heart, 'Jax' also went out of her way to help people in her community. Like me, she dealt with haters in spite of her good deeds. Jax was famous for seeing the light of Divinity in everyone, including the ex-con who became her boyfriend. Looking past a rap sheet that included burglary, robbery and assault, believing in the good of humanity to turn itself around, she invested in helping him. Whether convinced or conned, my sweet friend invited him to move into her beautiful 6,000 square foot home. That was when her jewelry started disappearing. Coincidentally, his taste for heroin appeared. She gave him more chances than he deserved to turn it around only to be let down again. She'd finally had enough and was ready to give him the boot. Good for her!

Then her house burned down. Everything she owned was lost in the fire. Well, it seemed that way, at first. The most important thing missing was Jax. Not a trace, not a word.

If she was in trouble, she knew she could always call on me. Granted, we had stopped talking shortly before the fire. I got triggered when she yelled at me for missing an appointment. I don't do well with being yelled at. I would have given anything to make amends, but the phone never rang. The police put out a missing person bulletin. Where did she go, and why?

Months of hand-wringing and kicking myself for letting such a small thing come between us finally came to a close. Found by demolition workers, not police dogs, her decomposing remains were discovered wrapped in plastic, buried in a shallow grave under her house.

Traffic cameras caught the ex-con driving her Jeep. It was filled with expensive equipment and her jewelry. He'd just come from the pawn shop. Funny how those items weren't in the blaze, huh? It sure looked pre-meditated to me. Her salon's polish remover was used to torch the house, and they arrested him for arson.

Arson. That's IT?! That was all they had on the creep. Arson. Although his dirtbag lawyer was succeeding with "lack of evidence to prosecute for murder," justice prevailed with guilty charges on all accounts. They both tried to get away with murder. I wonder how that lawyer faces himself in the mirror every morning. Then again, people like that don't have a reflection.

My heart goes out to her and her family. *God, why it is that horrible people get to live, even profit off murder, while beautiful souls are brutally robbed of life?* It doesn't matter if you call it fate, destiny or karma, in the end, it's a crying shame.

You just never know when your last words are your final comments. *I'll see you in heaven, Jax . With love, Patsy.*

# *Three*

My mother never learned to drive. She tried, once. We had to replace a lot of trash cans that day. As if it were the car's fault, she got out, slammed the door and said, "See? THIS is why I don't drive!" With seven kids, she had built-in chauffeurs, so that worked out. For all her hard work, Mom deserved to be driven around.

Once all the kids were gone, my mother got her first real job. "You'd have thought she was working for the president," my sister Meg said. It was a boring key punch job, but for Mom, it was everything. Meg was bored out of her mind, but Mom couldn't be happier with a simple job, people who adored her, and money of her own. She was in heaven on a daily basis. It's no wonder she thought my life was chaotic. By comparison, mine was insanity on steroids.

Back then, women were 'allowed' to be mothers, nurses, teachers or receptionists. But first, marriage and kids, of course. In a million years, I never expected to someday be the owner of a construction business in New Jersey. Women just didn't act 'that way.'

Thankfully, one high school teacher changed my life with his enthusiasm for business. It opened my eyes to a whole new world of possibilities. With a knack for numbers, the class was easy to ace. Every class was easy, actually. I was that weird combination of super-smart and party girl, if you know what I mean?

One marriage, two sons, and my accounting degree later, Ray wanted me to be a stay-at-home mother. Great idea. Really bad timing. The union paychecks kept us living hand-to-mouth and eating pasta too many times a week. If we accepted this as our destiny, then we were destined to fail. Going back to my $45/hr job was out of the question. That wasn't what my husband wanted.

Before you laugh, remember that a child learns what she lives. My mother's ways became my ways: whatever my husband wanted is what I supported. "When in Rome" as the saying goes. Plus, I happen to like being an old school wife.

However, I had to take the reins. With a hundred bucks and *'no more pasta!'* in my head, every vacant commercial building in three counties got a business card or a flyer. One phone call, one interview, and one 50% deposit on a $300k job later, it was one wonderful day, let me tell you.

Next day, we showed up on the job in a new truck, with new tools, a new gang box, and one shocked owner who said, "Looks like I just got someone started in business!" I said, "Yessir, you have, and you won't regret it." Pardon the pun, but we nailed the job and never looked back. Finally, Ray's employment income would be more than unemployment income.

We took charge of our destiny. That's the power of a decision. I got to work from home, grow the business *and* be the full time mother/wife Ray envisioned. Was it all sunshine and roses? Hell, no. You have to be a professional plate-spinner to keep it all up in the air and working, man. It is trial-by-fire, big time. But there was no other way to kick karma's ass - the union wasn't giving us meatballs for day-old spaghetti leftovers, now were they?

Life was never dull. We *tried* to keep it to a dull roar, but hey, there are certain 'issues' that just come with the job. To an outsider, it probably looked as if we were human magnets drawing missiles to our heads. That was especially true for my mother. In her eyes, we signed up for chaos.

I can still picture Mom's thick, pink and white framed eyeglasses, perched on the end of her nose; a cigarette dangling from the side of her mouth. "Hi, Ma! I just came by to see how you are!"

I tried to be bubbly. She'd seen enough grief for three lifetimes. In fact, Mom was the only person left in her family. Refusing to bend under the weight of a difficult life, she became famous for saying, "Life is for the living. If you're not living, you don't have a life."

Apparently, we knew how to live, but maybe just a bit too much for her liking.

"Ohhh, it's y-o-u. You always got *somethin'* going on. What's the story today??" That rocking chair would creek forward, and I would cringe. "Ma, I didn't do nuttin' I swear."

# Four

The doorbell rang at dinnertime. We weren't expecting company.

I half-opened the door. "May I help you?"

"Are you Patricia Miller, owner of RPM Construction?"

*Oh God, now what?*

"We need to have a word with you and your husband. When would now be a good time for you?"

"Patty! Get back in here! Tell whoever it is we are eatin' and they can call before they come next time!" Ray wasn't happy. Neither were these men.

I tried to keep calm. "Babe, hang on a second, I think this is important." Some things you just sense, ya know?

Turns out it was a personal visit from the mafia, I mean, uh, the president of the New Jersey carpenter's union. A few thugs, I mean, 'associates,' stood at his side. They'd been after us for years - ever since the day we went independent and started kicking ass in three states.

"Ma'am, we need you to be part of the union." The "...or else" was implied. We'd heard they were pissed off at how many jobs we were taking from them as a non-union company. He *greatly encouraged* us to return to the union. The threat of losing Ray's union book, meaning he would lose his pension after being vested 100%, was put lightly as our 'incentive.' How could we say no?

The upside is that being a union contractor allowed us to build some great buildings in NJ. We framed and fit out most of the buildings that the average person uses on a daily basis. Retail stores, medical facilities, office buildings, schools as well as entire strip malls, all from the ground up.

One that stood out was an assisted living facility located in Englishtown, NJ. Our company had the finish carpentry and door installation package on this project. With over 2,000 doors to install, it would be months of work.

We called the union hall for help. They sent over two older carpenters and two younger apprentices. Dave was one of the apprentices who was eager to learn, and took a strong liking to Ray.

Ray learned his craft the old fashioned way. Sure, his family connections could have facilitated buying his way into the union, but that wasn't Ray's style. He learned by partnering with the oldest carpenters. It's a smart person who learns from other people. Ray capitalized on the chance to gain all their trade secrets.

So, with Dave newly in awe of Ray's skills, he became Ray's apprentice. Pay it forward. In turn, Dave was loyal like a dog.

Maybe too loyal....

It was a Thursday morning, late spring, and the day after payday. We always started at 7am; Ray would always call me on break about two hours later. That day, however, the phone rang early. It was only 7:30am. Ray was laughing on the other end.

"What's wrong?" I said.

"Oh, you are never going to believe this one."

It could have been anything. I held my breath and prayed.

"Dave's here and I can't get him to leave."

"OK. Why does he have to leave?" *Oh God, what now?* My mind was reeling with possibilities.

"Well, he said he is here to work, which is great. Problem is, he isn't wearing any pants." Ray laughed harder and harder trying to describe this 300lb young man wearing a tool belt over his tight white briefs."Pat, he is still drunk, and he has a bloody lip."

"What in the actual fuck, Ray?"

"I know, right? We've got...a 300lb hungover apprentice...(more laughing and gasping)...with a bloody lip...wearing a *toolbelt* over his tighty whitey's, who wants to work!" More hysterics.

Apparently Dave went on a bender the night before. He tried to go home and shower for work, but his father beat the shit out of him, then locked him out. So Dave, being the loyal dog he was, insisted on coming to the job. On the way, he took off his bloodstained jeans and arrived ready to go wearing just briefs and work boots. Talk about loyalty.

Ray said, "Dude, you have to leave. You can't stay here and work in your underwear!" Dave flatout refused. "Pat, you gotta call the business agent at the union hall. Have him come to the site and remove Dave."

Well, that was awkward. I made the call to Billy the BA and explained the situation to him.

After he stopped laughing he promised to head over and handle it for us. Fortunately, he arrived with some clothes for Dave and was able to convince him to leave the site, tools in tow. After the owners saw that 'display' there was no way we could have Dave back on the job, pants or no pants.

We laughed about Dave for years. We have him to thank, as well. He proved we needed to change paydays from Wednesday to Friday. 'Work hard, play harder' is pretty typical in construction: when the men get paid they tend to go drinking with their newfound money. As a result, the following day they pulled a lot of no-shows, or, in Dave's case, too much of a show. No more chances. Now, if they want to party it up they have Saturday to sleep it off and all day Sunday to find their pants.

Another time, my phone ran earlier than usual. With so many moving parts, and people in the mix, the job can feel like a professional babysitting gig. Something wasn't right; it was just too early to be breaking up a fight between the subs already.

"Hey, uh, Pat, there's been a bad accident. We were coming home from Atlantic City at 4AM, you know, and there was this guy on the road..."

*Oh God. What now?*

"Well, we was coming over a big hill, and all of a sudden there's this guy parked in the fast lane, half on the shoulder, half on the road and we, uh, we hit him going 80 and cut him in half, Pat. It was an accident, I swear!"

That's exactly what it was: an accident, off the clock. Period, end of story. When I got the summons to appear in court, I thought it was a joke. What the hell was going on?

Well, it seemed the victim's common law wife got herself a shark lawyer to sue *me* for millions in a work-related wrongful death suit. My own insurance company jumped ship. *They* assigned fault, stepped-off and left me hanging in the breeze. Tell me again what insurance is for?

That woman's lawyer was looking to own my house, trucks and equipment, then give the widow a percent of his killing. It didn't matter that the dead guy was drunk, parked half on the highway, changing a tire in the dark. It didn't matter that *none of this was relevant.* I was an easy target and they had dollar signs for pupils.

"Judge, I didn't tell my guys to carpool. They weren't on the clock. This isn't my company's fault or my wrongdoing." The five million dollar lawsuit should have been dismissed but noooo…

"That may be Mrs. Miller, but I'd like to hear the whole story. I rule it to go to discovery. I'm just curious how this whole thing happened and will allow it to move forward if only to satisfy my own personal interest."

*Wait, what?!*

The prosecuting attorney took my lawyer to the side and sneered, "Why didn't you just tell her to say she wanted them to carpool as part of the job that day? This would have been an open-and-shut case covered by her insurance."

"Oh, so you want me to recommend my client perjure herself on the stand, is that it?"

There's no way I would have lied. Sure, I had nothing to do with this case *at all,* and could have fibbed to get it handled, but why? When this was over I needed to have my integrity intact, even if no one else did.

That my insurance company abandoned me without there being a legal ruling was just wrong. Who were they to decide fault and drop representation, anyway? And so we went to court to satisfy a judge's curiosity at my expense: $80,000 worth of defense, out of pocket. They sent a representative to the courtroom every single day, taking notes and reporting back to the main office, though. For *that,* they had time and interest.

In the end, they got to report something no one saw coming: according to my attorney, this wrongful death suit changed New Jersey case law. From that day forward, insurance companies would be required to represent their clients from Day 1 and until such time as liability was determined.

I won the case and sent those deep pocket lawyers home crying. No millions for you, jerk-offs.

For anyone else, ever again in the future, the new case law will serve *their* vested interests until such time as liability is legally denied. To think that the judge's personal curiosity prompted all of this…that it was allowed to move forward based on his morbid interest in a grotesque car accident, proves how twisted the legal system truly is.

My attorney said, "You really ought to be a lawyer, Mrs. Miller."

"I'd be in contempt of court half the time. Besides, it is better to kick ass than to kiss it."

I rest my case.

Handling the entire nightmare of a case on my own was hard as hell. But we won, and I was damn proud of it.

How come this stuff never happens to other people? It's not like I was trying to make life hard. Construction, in general, is full of issues and people with issues who do construction.

Mom didn't seem to care. It was just another day in my wacky life.

"You need to get out of that damn business, Patricia. It's nothing but trouble. Go back to accounting. Grow somebody else's business like you did before, then go home and make dinner for your family. It doesn't have to be that hard."

"But Ma, this is what Ray and I do. We built this business from the ground up. You know that. I can't just walk away. Ray is counting on me to run the books and keep growing the business. We deal with bullshit just like everybody else."

"*Yours* just never ends." She took another drag on her cigarette and in one puff, ended the conversation.

# Five

She was right: there was always something. The way I see it though, there's always something to learn no matter what happens, no matter how bad it gets. If we don't learn the lesson, we are bound to repeat it. It's like finding the light switch in your darkest hour. It might take a year, or years, to find the damn thing, but if you do find the value in the experience, you grow your own set of wings. No one else can help you 'Phoenix up' and get the hell out of those ashes. And you know what? You may never know *why* something happened. Things happen that are not our fault, but they become our responsibility.

Orthodox Jews believe "measure according to measure." Because you drowned others you were drowned, and in the end those who drowned you will be drowned. Pretty literal stuff. Does the person who drowned you, because you drowned someone else, then get drowned, too? Where does the karmic liability cycle actually end?

To others, the meaning of karma is not a form of punishment or reward from a past life. It is life, right now, wheelin' and dealin' both good and bad hands of cards at us. Fate means you can't change the cards you're dealt. Future karma is generated by your response. And destiny is created as a result of managing those hands. Good card players can win a bad hand as much as bad card players can lose winning hands.

I know, hiking the Andes in flip-flops might seem easier than managing the obstacles thrown your way. Boy, do I get it. Oye, the blisters! Do you curse your shoes? The path? The steepness of the mountains? Or do you find gratitude for the fresh air, peace and gorgeous views as you massage your tired feet?

What we want is for the road traveled to be worth the miles. Sometimes, it takes a bit of time to see the value of a jerk, or an injustice thrown in your lap. Sometimes, it is merely stating the obvious lesson learned at the hands of some real cutthroat card sharks.

I wrote this 'hindsight letter' over coffee the other morning. It came quickly. I think it's a sign of growth to not want to ear-box some of these people. Well, I might still *want* to, but…

*How people treat you is their karma; how you react is*

*yours.*

*- Wayne Dyer*

*THANK YOU…*

*Thank you to the doubters, the haters, the envious and the jealous for pushing me to prove that I could do it.*

*Thank you to those who doubted I could run a construction company alone after my husband's death. I discovered I could and I did it twice as good. You taught me strength and perseverance.*

*Thank you to those who looked down upon me with sorrow and pity. You taught me to dig deep and not allow myself to be a victim.*

*Thank you to the high school hockey club haters who despised me for taking control and running shit better than it had ever been done before. You're welcome for raising tens of thousands of dollars, getting you a home rink, matching uniforms and a team banner. You taught me to ignore the critics when you're in charge of positive transformations.*

*Thank you to the Super who called me while my husband was on hospice and threatened to take my contract back if I wasn't personally onsite to run the job by the following Friday. You forced me to persevere and show up in a time of darkness. In an odd, weird way it helped me deal with grief…thank you.*

*Thank you to developers who have mistreated me, bullied me with their power, and taken opportunities from me because I didn't cower down to their power. I learned to accept that they were keeping me from other opportunities. When one door closes another one opens. I kept my principles in tact.*

*Thank you to the married corporate executives who wanted me to be their side piece. I found the strength and dignity to say no, only to suddenly lose hundreds of thousands in work opportunities. I kept my reputation and self respect intact.*

*Thank you to corporate America, NY Life in particular, for not paying my husband's life insurance policy because he died 7 days too early to avoid contestability. You taught me not to chase blood money, and to earn my own.*

*Thank you to the Catholic Church, Sister Blanche at St.Thomas in Old Bridge particularly, for physically abusing me until my hands bled because I was left handed. You taught me to stay true to myself and not to change for anyone, even during times of pain.*

*Thank you to my wealthy relatives who didn't spare a dime to a Go Fund Me campaign my nephew set up to help me pay medical bills. You taught me that strangers can be kinder and more generous than your own blood. I learned that being related doesn't come with an obligation to like someone.*

*Thank you to my ex-boyfriend, Rick, who was a narcissist, user, thief, liar and cheater. You taught me that I can't fix everyone, even though I can see their potential. I learned to let go and let God take over. Thanks to you, my life has taken on a level of spiritual awakening I didn't know was possible.*

*Thank you to all of my friends who disappeared during the 2 years of my husband's suffering with cancer. You voluntarily removed yourself from my life. You taught me that those who you think are loyal are not, they're only around to benefit. Yet, sometimes the people you least expect to be loyal are there for you every day. You taught me to pay attention to the details in life, for there are many signs and synchronicities flashed before us everyday.*

*Thank you to some of my family members who taught me to set boundaries. I learned that I can't keep everyone happy and sometimes, no matter what I did, it could never be enough.*

It is entirely possible friends and family felt the same way about me: that they couldn't do enough in my eyes, and yet, few requests for help came from my mouth. The years of stress, built-up frustrations and losses could have easily colored my own filters, making it hard for me to see the ways others wanted to reach out. Still, it would have been nice if someone offered to walk the dog while I sat with Mom, Dad or Ray in the emergency room, *again*.

In the end, in an effort to pull the positive out of piles of shit, the truth is you can't be the light and hold another in darkness. It just doesn't work that way. However, there is such a thing as casting your pearls before swine. Time is the one thing no one can get back. Waste not, want not.

This is my year for setting boundaries and exercising "tough love." It is a huge challenge to let go of fixing, and set my foot down to employees, friends, family or gossipy bitches with nothing better to do than run me down. I'm done with hearing that I didn't give enough, pay enough, or try hard enough. Like Liz says, "If Pat writes you off, you've really messed-up." The bane of a fixer is the temptation to help - you want to help, but it goes beyond that, trickling into fixing. I'm trying to be done with that…to see who is really in need and who is trying to soak me with a smile on their dial.

As for the men who think I'm a frail 50-something widow who is 'getting her sexy on' for the first time in years? Boys, you may see small feet in mile-high heels, but back of them is a pair of work boots with steel toes. Don't piss down my back then tell me it's raining And, get your grubby hand outta my pocket.

I swear, if I had a magic wand, I would silence the mouths of the liars, freeze the hands of thieves, and make all the players' dicks limp for life.

# Six

I was up late, sipping wine and trying to get sleepy, when this commercial came on. Here's how I heard it: *Did a creepy priest put his hands, or worse, on you? It's time to do something about that prick. Call us now to be part of a class action lawsuit. You may get millions for your suffering. Call 1-800- LAWYERS. Sharks are standing by.*

I hated to admit it, but the Catholic church scars left me feeling a wee bit victimized, even after all these years. I smiled and dialed.

"Hello, Ma'am. Were you sexually abused by a priest? Would you like to file a claim? What's your story? Tell us all about it. You could be awarded money for it!"

I could hear him salivating on the other end of the line.

"No, I was physically abused by a nun and *I want my money*!! I had welts for years because of that horrible woman. I want to know what you're going to do about it."

"Well, Ma'am, that's next. We are building a case against sexually-inappropriate priests right now. The nuns are on our list. Call us back when you see that ad." He was clearly disappointed. One less shark fed that night.

"Sure, I'll call back. Lemme guess, 1-800-SUE-A-NUN?"

The line went dead. I figured there wasn't enough money for the lawyers to care about bleeding hands caused by some penguin in a habit who developed the habit of beating kids bloody out in the hallway. The way her eyes lit up proved I wasn't the one with the devil in them. Strangely coincidental that 'evil' and 'devil' are just one letter apart. Does the "d" stand for 'defending evil'?

My mother, the Eucharist minister, cushioned the Catholic church, saying, "You can't be angry at the Lord for what people do." I heard this daily as she handed me one of Dad's handkerchiefs to throw up in. The mere sight of school and I was tossing my cookies. Did God really only love right-handed people? No wonder St. Jude was my favorite saint. Mom made sure we remained faithful. We did, but it was 'kicking and screaming' compliance.

Dad's nickname was "Lefty." I wonder how much abuse he took for being left-handed? He left school in seventh grade. I'll bet he was motivated by all the 'nunsense' too. Just sayin'...

A few years later, he met my mother at a Catholic wedding in Jersey City. Perfect. Mom was a New York City girl. When they got married, he said, "Let's move to the country." Think Zsa Zsa Gabor in "Green Acres," complete with a tiny, remotely located farmhouse. Poor Mom. Where's the bus? Where are the trains? Where are the shops? Why do we have to wait for it to rain to have well water?

Mom accepted that her destiny was the wife of a stressed-out man, six kids, and country living. She hand-washed cloth diapers, fell asleep with a baby in her arms and a bottle boiling over on the stove. Somehow, in all that chaos, she was the most loving, dedicated Moma kid could hope for.

Then trouble came. I mean *real trouble*. Baby number seven was on the way and not expected to live.

"Mrs. Ferrano, I highly recommend that you abort this child." I don't care if you are wearing a white coat and stethoscope, you just don't open a conversation that way to a devout Catholic mother. There had been complications, heavy bleeding at five months, and big concerns that I, lucky number seven, wasn't going to see the light of day.

"Sir, I will do nothing of the sort to this child."

He persisted, "Your baby will be deformed. She will have…" He trailed off.

"What? What will this baby have, doc?!"

"Mrs. Ferrano, it's likely your baby will suffer with low IQ and developmental disorders."

Without missing a beat, my mother disagreed, "There will be no abortions in my family. This baby, like all the others, will be fine, thank you very much."

"If you don't get off your feet for the next four months you will lose that child, Cathy. And even then…"

"I got this, Doc."

With that, my mother crushed out her cigarette, turned on her heel, and took to the bed; not an easy feat with six kids to feed and an alcoholic husband. Unlike Zsa Zsa, who would have turned skirt for the city, Mom dug in her heels to make sure I survived. She was determined to prove Doc wrong.

A house full of kids and hungry mouths to feed was beyond stressful. Dad did his best, but back then, 'best' also included a lot of drinking. It's what men did after work. Every single day. Into the night. Isn't it funny I ended-up working in a field known for alcoholics? Hmmm.

Mom ran interference between us when Dad was on another bender. She couldn't always be there, though. Sometimes he would drag us out of bed at 4am to clean the house he just wrecked. Isolated, she had no one to turn to. Her classy family wouldn't hear of her staying with an alcoholic, so she said nothing. She couldn't leave him, and did her best to protect us from him.

Meg nicknamed Mom the "Slipper Ninja." She could clip the back of your leg without getting up from the chair. She never physically hit us, but those tea cups didn't exactly feel good, either. A sharp shooter from her rocking chair, Mom never missed her target. Nice. It's a wonder she didn't take up drinking, too.

Against all odds, I was born five weeks early.

So there we were, four boys in one bedroom, three girls in the other. Was it a karmic debt that seven kids found themselves dirt-poor, competing for attention and food? Did our souls actually need the challenge of sleeping with rats, or hoping for more than a can of corn for school lunch? Was this to teach us all something? If it was, we all took away different lessons. Some of my siblings are still in reaction to those experiences. Instead of moving on, they carry the load, and have let their past define, rather than shape, who they are to this day.

Maybe mom's fortitude was passed on to us kids? The strength to get through horrendous conditions, a dirt-poor environment, abuse, grief, loss and the resulting determination to find joy anyway, in any way you can, must have been passed on, too. At least, that's the story I tell myself.

Thinking that I picked not only a difficult childhood but also a life of challenges brings comfort somehow; it means that all this bullshit wasn't just random at all, but rather, a well-designed 'training' event for what was to come.

However, nothing can prepare you for catching your husband's intestines in your bare hands. Yeah, so that happened...

The doctors dubbed it my "Vietnam Life," saying veterans of three wars haven't seen the 'action' I've seen.

"How can you be so calm?" they would say.

"What do you want me to do, bawl my eyes out in the hallway?!"

A fireman doesn't mourn the blaze, he fights it. Thank you, Mom, for instilling so much fight in your baby girl. Apparently, I needed it.

*"It ain't about how hard you hit. It's about how hard you can get hit and keep moving forward. It's about how much you can take, and keep moving forward.*
*That's how winning is done!"*

*- Sylvester Stallone in Rocky Balboa*

# Seven

Funny how one person, in one day, can completely change the world. Your world. Your family's world. Your future. That's what happened when Frank the farmer came by to see if Dad wanted to buy his leftover tomato and corn baskets. Dad agreed, stuck the baskets out on the roadside, and everything sold out in a few hours. It wasn't long before we opened a farm market, reselling Frank's produce from a single table's worth to a panel truck full of produce.

That day was a mixed blessing, though. I didn't get to spend my summers like all the other kids my age. No, instead, we were up before sunrise to get produce from the local farms and haul it all back to our farm store. Hefting sacks of potatoes is hard for a five year old, but doing it all in the summer sun was brutal.

Customers used to hate it when I served them because I was really, really good at math. Unlike my sisters, who rounded-up or down to make it easy, I would calculate down the ounce what the cost of those potatoes would be. By then, I was a seasoned, hard-working eight year old who felt we deserved every penny for our efforts. Customers would challenge me and Dad would smile and say, "Oh yes, I'm sure you're right, sir, but why don't you have her show you how she got that amount, then just pay her because she's always right."

*Awww, thanks, Pop.* He always told me I was special.

Fifteen years and two college degrees later, I was *specialized,* earning $45 an hour for that 'knack' - a lot of money in the early 80's. It would come in handy later whenever a grown-ass man tried to put his grubby little hand in my pocket, too.

Was the farm market our punishment? Words like karma, fate and destiny don't mean shit to a kid that just wants to have summertime fun, man. It was hard to imagine the value of working like a slave when everybody else got to go play. Did it teach us to have a work ethic? Sure. Did we get the real lesson at age five? Hardly. Was being poor as hell the real burden? You betcha. Duly noted.

I'll never forget the sight of my aunt's massive gold Seville coming across the horizon. It was loaded-down with beach-bound cousins and second-hand clothes. For some reason, in spite of our need for donated clothes, they thought *we* were the rich side of the family. Ha. Try sharing one bathroom with eight other people and see how rich you feel. They had no idea what it was like for seven kids to clamor for air space and food. Dad was a chauvinist who felt boys should eat first. The girls had to wait while the boys either demolished or hid what was left of a box of cereal. Everyday was a fight for attention, food, and underwear.

We were so poor I had to wear my brother's underwear. That hole in front didn't do anything but make me cry. The wind rustled through that puppy with every swish of my skirt. The worst part: no one would tell me what that hole was for.

Our cousins didn't know what went on; all they saw was us having fruit fights and laughing all the time. Lots of shit happened that nobody knew about. Out there in the country, if no one else saw it, it didn't happen. Let me just tell you now, it did. With Lefty's tirades that may, or may not, result in somebody getting their ass beat, life in the country wasn't all it was cracked up to be. Of course, our cousins never heard those bits. As kids, we just thought it was normal to hide out in the woods until Dad sobered up, so why would we say something?

Lefty declined all invitations to visit the beach house. We were too busy making money, after all. At least, that was the impression he wanted them to have. Later in life he admitted, "If you kids had seen the beach, if you knew better, you would have wanted better." We didn't need to see the beach to know we wanted better, trust me.

The upside of working the farm stand was that me and my sisters got one helluva good education in running a business. In fact, of the seven, it's the three of us who became successful entrepreneurs. You could say it was our fate. If there is any truth to "meant to be," apparently we were meant to learn how to buy, price, sell and handle money. What's cool is that we all have this amazing photographic memory: if we see it, hear it, or are shown it, we immediately learn it.

My father grilled it into my tiny head that I was special; that I was born to do something special. It sure helped balance all the times I felt left out. I still had one burning question, though. "Hey, Ma, how come there aren't any baby pictures of me?"

She matter-of-factly said, "By the time we got through Baby #5, we weren't trying so hard to capture baby's first steps, Patty. I was already too busy trying to manage all the other kids. By the time you came along, we knew what a baby girl looked like at age one, and beyond. It wasn't new or novel. Pictures just weren't a priority anymore."

*Oh, you mean the rose was off the bloom, huh?* There's hardly a photo of me anywhere. I felt like the forgotten child. You'd think 'miracle baby' might rank but no, not so much. It was enough for them that I wasn't born deformed, and made it into the world without Mom dying in the process. 'Special' didn't require photos.

By the time I was old enough to get handed-down a car like all my brothers and sisters, it never happened. Dad was burned out on six other kids wrecking cars, DUIs and inflated insurance costs. I paid the price for their issues by getting no help buying a car. So, I saved and bought my first car all on my own. The whole, "I can do it myself" attitude got an early start in life. I *had* to do it myself…and I did.

I remember sitting in my new car like it was yesterday. What an awesome feeling. The radio played real good. That was all I could do with my new car: sit in the driveway for three months, listening to the radio, until I could afford car insurance. I laugh when my brothers and sisters say I had it easier than them. Ha. I paid for their mistakes more than a few times. As unfair as that felt, I learned to make my own way.

Thankfully, Dad got sober. I'm not sure he meant to, but while helping the oldest, Jimmy, get through AA, he jumped on the wagon, too. After that, he was a kind, funny, and strict, but loving father. He also knew stuff we couldn't imagine being true. He would say, "Turn off that spigot! Some day you're going to have to pay for bottled water, mark my words." I know our well ran dry, but dang, this was in the 60s. How the hell did he know that someday we would be buying bottled water? There was only one reasonable explanation: Lefty was a time-traveler. Well, that's what I thought as a kid.

I wasn't the only one who got lucky with the timing of Dad's sobriety. All my brothers and sisters had to wait until they were 17 to date. Heck, we couldn't even get our ears pierced until we were eighteen. Dad was super strict about a *lot* of things.

But there I was, age 16, taken with a cutie named Ray. I'm sure I thought I could help him. Being a fixer starts early in life. Not only did I fall for him, I felt for him. His mother literally dumped him and his brother on their father's doorstep one day. I couldn't imagine growing up knowing your mother rang the doorbell and scrammed, for starters. But to leave two tiny boys with an abusive alcoholic father, and not to come back, not call, not nothing, for years and years? That's a cold piece of steel right there, man.

Ray wound up at a makeshift home for boys. Twenty boys crammed together in a few rooms, sleeping in nasty bunk beds, dealing with bugs and abuse. It might have been a good hideout from his father's place, but as the lesser of two evils, it was still a living hell.

Sometimes, people genuinely need to be rescued. We lost count how many times my sister Meg drove 40 minutes just to bring Ray to our house for a little while.

Thankfully, Mom and Dad took him in for good one day. He arrived with all his worldly possessions stuffed into a dirty old pillowcase. You'd have thought he was a homeless orphan. So, yes, as unorthodox as it was to have my boyfriend move in, my parents took him in. The scrappy 16 year old might not have made it much longer if it weren't for my parents helping him to beat karma's ass.

P.S. It wouldn't be the first time we helped save Ray's life.

# *Eight*

I might have known, just watching the cake fall over on our wedding day, that life with Ray was going to be challenging right from "I do." Tonight was no different.

Ray was an architectural artist in his own right. Drawing diagrams on dinner napkins, he would explain them to me as I tried to clear our dinner plates. Building steel frame structures all over New Jersey was *his* job. I did the books, built the business from the backend, and had no intention of ever being boots on the ground.

My life was one long laundry list after *my* 10-hour day. Do the dishes. Get the boys onto their homework. Make Ray's lunch for the next day. Send out the 1099s. Cancel that concrete order. Order more steel studs. Tell that guy his change order was messed-up and he still owes us $45k. Organize a fundraiser for the high school ice hockey team. Get sponsors. Beg for raffle prizes. Get some rest. If I wasn't so wired, I'd be tired. Wait, I was tired. All the time.

I nodded at him, then bolted for the kitchen. "Can't we just have a normal dinner, Ray? We worked all damn day and now you want to keep working?"

"You are going to need to know how to do this someday, so sit down and shut up!" Dishes be damned, I pulled out a chair and sat my tired ass back down at the table.

Wasn't I doing enough already? I was the oh-so-dedicated homemaker, involved parent, loving wife and hella-good cook, from scratch, just like Mom. I put up with Ray's short temper, clipped words and possessiveness, too. I would tell myself, *Just smile. You love him. He loves you. This is how couples do, right?*

"I made it too easy for your father, Patty." Mom confessed this long after we'd all moved into lives of our own. That's what women did back then. Dad didn't have to do anything but bring home a paycheck. Granted, it was stressful. There were a lot of mouths to feed. Mom did such an amazing job that he had no idea what it took to get everything done; that dirty diapers can't wait, and hungry bellies have loud voices. He was oblivious to it all, by Mother's design. "I created a monster," Mom admitted.

Children learn what they live. I married a facsimile of my father, right down to being a protege: once I was Dad's; apparently now I was Ray's. I didn't remember signing up for this. Harumpf! I sat down with attitude. I know, I know, the "good wife" supports her man. And my support was where, exactly?

Then Ray would remind us with his patented, inevitable, end-all be-all rebuttal, "You guys are gonna miss me when I'm gone." Oh, just cue the family eye roll one more time, will ya? We'd been hearing this for a while now, and it was getting old.

Yet, there were other times, like tonight, when I wondered, *Is he leaving us?* It sure seemed that way. If those psychics told him about anybody dying he was forbidden to share it with me. I just didn't want to know. I stuck to my patron saint of hopeless cases and prayed for the best while he got his cards read on the regular. I was OK with that. *Just don't tell me what they said.* I didn't want to know the future, especially negative stuff. Today was a scramble and tomorrow would be more of the same. I didn't need to know if anybody close was gonna die anytime soon. My brain was tired and my body was on autopilot. *Must. Do. Laundry.*

Ray slapped the table. "Hey! Pay attention. This is important!" My to-do list would have to wait. He was home for the night and had a full agenda planned out, laundry-be-damned. White flag. When in Rome, do what the Romans do.

"Patty, remember this one thing: if you can bid it, you can build it."

"OK, Ray, tell me again how that soffit fits around the duct work. I mean, the storefront pipes." Sigh. He put on glasses to read the blueprint to me...all 95 pages of it. Interpreting a blueprint, searching for design flaws, creating options for the clients, and accurate labor cost assessments were all part of the bid process. Working 60-80 hour weeks, our business was doing really well in part because he was so good at this initial stage.

"You can write our address in pen now. The Moving Millers have settled-in," I said to Dad. We did so well that we moved to a secluded home in the country. I know, that is a strangely familiar story, huh? At least we had running water. It was perfect for raising kids and, since deer don't gossip, life was *really* good.

Ray and I were in the office estimating new projects. It was a hot August day and we were in the bidding phase of our construction business. It's a vital, and super-stressful part of getting work. The kids were home from school, playing in the pool. It was lunchtime and Subway got the most votes.

So, off I went to Subway to pick up some subs. What I didn't know was that this trip would become a memory that would last a lifetime, and not in the best ways imaginable.

Got the subs, headed for home. We were hungry and I couldn't wait to get back.

Rounding the corner, on the home stretch, I see my neighbor Carmela standing in the middle of my street screaming my name, "PASQUALINA! PASQUALINA!" (Patricia in Italian.) She was waving her hands and crying hysterically.

I pulled halfway into her driveway and flung open my door. "What's wrong? What's wrong?!!"
All she could get out was, "Enzo, Enzo, Enzo!! In the house! Enzo!!" She pointed toward their house.

Enzo owned the local pizza parlor around the corner. He often stopped and chatted while he drove up and down the street, like a mayor might do.

He laughed it off and always said, "No, Pasqualina, *you* are the mayor. You were the first one on the block."

He was such a friendly, personable man; a real charmer with the ladies, me included. Loved that man.

I ran into the house. Enzo was lying on the kitchen floor. His face was purple. Carmela was screaming. Their son was bawling.

"What happened? What happened?!" I knew I had to give him mouth to mouth, but if he was choking the Heimlich was more appropriate.

Carmela could barely speak. "He. Was. Eating jello. He fell down."

"Somebody, give me a phone! Get me a telephone!!" I said.

The shock and hysteria caused so much panic that every phone was on the floor, shattered. Finally, his son found me a phone and I called 911. Being purple, I knew Enzo had been without oxygen for some time. They immediately dispatched an ambulance. Thank God for these people. They talked me through the process of what to do, and most of all, what not to do.

I was trying my best to save him when an eerie calm came over me. I felt like I was floating over my body and watching from above as I started to give Enzo mouth-to-mouth: turn his head, clear his mouth, now...

Oh my god. He gurgled, then suddenly, red Jello-O was strewn on the floor as it flowed out of his mouth. With every gurgle, red Jello-O came gushing out.

It was the same red Jello-O he'd been given two hours earlier for a stress test on his heart. He went in because he was convinced he was having heart issues - for *weeks*. His all-knowing doctor said, "You're fine." They sent him home, only to drop in his kitchen minutes later.

I tried to save him, pushing as much oxygen into him as I could. The louder he gurgled the more oxygen he got. I continued for 10 minutes waiting for the paramedics. It truly felt like 10 hours before they arrived. At least he had a faint pulse, again. They took him in the ambulance and continued with shock treatments.

My job was done. I took a deep breath, got back in the car, and continued home with soggy subs.

The key barely turned in the door when Ray said, "Where the fuck were you for an hour and a half??"

I said "Babe, you are never going to believe this..." Then, I lost it. I started shaking and crying. It finally hit me what just happened. Ray sat me down, hugged and calmed me to a light sob. I guess Enzo never fully recovered from all that damage to his heart. At least I gave his family 22 more days of life and a chance to have closure with him.

I couldn't stop crying at his wake. I felt so bad; so *guilty* I wasn't there sooner. It was as if I failed. I failed Enzo. I failed his family. I failed to save my friend. We are where we are supposed to be no matter how it turns out. The rest is up to God.

I never got an official thank you from the family, but I didn't need one. I did what I could for Enzo. He was my friend for life, but God had a different plan for him. Eventually, I learned to accept his death as God's will.

I know God saw what I did that day. That's all that matters to me. *Rest in peace, my friend.*

# Nine

Sure, Ray was sort of pushy when it came to teaching me his side of the business. At the time, it didn't make sense why he insisted I learn how to bid a job. I was "the voice" of RPM Construction, not the face. He didn't care. For some reason, he pushed to get me in the field. *When in Rome...* I got myself a pair of kick-ass steel toe boots, and started showing up on site. The men didn't know what to think. Women in construction delivered coffee not commands.

I would show up on the jobsite and yell at everybody. That's a newbie for ya. It didn't work out so well. Women are called bitches for being assertive or aggressive if that's what it takes to get the job done. Men, on the other hand, are called "leaders" for being aggressive. WTF. I got the job done, too. What's with discounting over gender?

The company we built had a reputation for quality workmanship and quality materials. I always say, "You can't make chicken salad taste good if you're starting out with chicken shit." We cut steel, not corners.

You're only as good as your last job; everybody checks references, and nobody gives a fuck what you built 20 years ago. Every time a job was done we were technically unemployed, looking for work. If you're new to the biz you'll practically work with, or for, anyone. But we earned the right to be picky.

Even so, it's a big industry, and we never knew who we were going to end up working beside; who hustled a low-bid for the job, and would be a pain in the ass to work with. With so many drunks, drug addicts, convicts and creeps in the business, walking the line between developing camaraderie and commanding the ship was a slippery slope for a woman.

I never knew what I was driving up to on the next new job.

On this particular day, I wasn't late, I was just driving fast. That's my M.O.: haul ass into a new jobsite, make a statement from the jump. Truth is, I haul ass everywhere. I love going fast. Anyway, I hit the brakes and spun out a little. It's my idea of a good time.

Dust clouds engulfed the jobsite trailer as I screeched to a stop. The trailer door flung open. I could barely see him, but could tell he was as wide as he was tall. "Whoa, whoaa, whoaaaaa, slow down cowgirl!" His thick Italian accent cut through the red clay dust and rocks. "You're coming in like your ass is on fire being chased by Injuns!"

Flashing my crooked smile, I walked into the trailer like I owned the place.

The squat man locked the door behind us. "I'm Joe. And who might *you* be?"

"Hey, nice to meet you, Joe. My name is Pat. I'm gonna be the framer here. How ya doin'?" I whipped out the paperwork and got right down to business. We were building a two-story office building in Brick, NJ, from the ground up. Joe would be doing all the site work and utilities on the job. We would be seeing a lot of each other. Working with Joe was gonna be a blast.

As I got up to leave, though, he stopped us both real short, before the door. He put his hand up, looked at my boots, looked back up and scowled. Whoa. Didn't see that coming.

In that thick Italian accent of his he blurted out, "Are you a fuckin' fed?! Are you a fed, Patty??! If you're a fucking fed, tell me *right now*!!" His cheeks were flushed. I thought he might collapse.

Jerking his left pant leg up he said, "I already got a fucking German Shepherd on my ankle. I don't need any more problems! Are you here to tap on me? Is that it? Is that why you're here?! Tell me now!" Joe reached for desk to steady himself. It wasn't easy for a squat man to reach his pant leg.

I laughed it off. "No, I'm not a fed, not a narc and will never be a narc. I gotta know, Joe, what the fuck did you do to get an ankle bracelet on you?"

He looked at the ground in an aw-shucks kinda way, then said, "Well, I asked people to do things that the feds found a little offensive."

"Joe, you don't have to worry about me. I stay out of people's business. I grew up in the 80s...I don't know nuttin'."

As the job progressed, Joe grew fond of me and Ray. We would often have breaks and lunches together with him in the trailer, telling stories and laughing our asses off. I will never forget the day we got onto the subject of past lives and psychics. My husband always went to psychics. I didn't mind, but I made him promise not to tell me if death was being forecast for people we knew. Why taint the present with future worries? Past life readings were on the table, of course. They had no bearing on today...or so I thought.

Ray had been intrigued by a birthmark on the back of his calf. It was a bright red, perfect triangle.

"You see this birthmark, Joe?"

"Yah, I see it, Raymond." Joe craned to see the tattoo-like birthmark.

"Well, apparently, in my last life, I was a Roman warrior who took an arrow to the back of the calf during a battle. The psychic said I brought that scar forward into this lifetime." Ray paused to see how the story landed. This wasn't our typical lunchtime B.S. session.

Joe froze, and, slowly drawing hand to chin, he stared Ray up and down, up and down. Time seemed to stand still before we heard his thick I'talian accent. "You know what, Raymond? You *doooo* look regal." He stepped back and scanned Ray some more, then said, "Where the fuck did you put King Arthur's roubles?! I know you have them if you were a fucking Roman warrior, Raymond. Where the fuck are the roubles??"

We were *howling*. Tears rolled down our cheeks. You couldn't have written a funnier skit.

It must have made Joe relax. I mean, old school I'talian men like that just don't discuss the paranormal on the regular. Then he said, "Do you believe in UFOs, Raymond?"

"Of course I do. I believe I got stabbed in the back of my calf with a fucking arrow on a battlefield in my last life…how could I not believe in UFOs, Joe?"

"Good, 'cuz I saw one on the Taaams Riva." (That would be the Toms River if Joe weren't quite so I'talian.) "I was in my boat and this fuckin' silver ting landed on the river right in front of me. I had a little wine that night, but I didn't have enough to see fucking UFOs."

We were dying with laughter.

I said, "Oh yeah, Joe? Did they levitate you to the mothership and do sexual experiments on ya?"

"I don't remember, Pat, but if they did they would have said 'WTF kind of sample human is this? Throw him back on the boat. We don't need no stinking Italian full of pasta and wine.'"

"Joe, stop! You're *killing* me!"

"Nah," he sez, "but if you eva ate my mudda-in-law's cooking you might die. I gotta shit in the bathtub everytime I eat her food, Patty."

"What the fuck? "Shit in the bathtub"? Does that mean your toilet is broken?" I didn't get it at all.

With red cheeks and his deepest cigar voice, he gravely said, "No, Patty, that's a saying in my I'talian family. It means you have to shit so much you need a bath tub large enough to hold it."

*How bad was the cooking that his family used that expression?*

He goes, "You know what? I like you kid. You're a good person with a good heart and great personality. Don't ever lose that sense of humor you got, kid…it will get you through life." He oughta know. People like him just know how to make the hard times funny, and the good times even better.

For years after the job ended, ol' Joe sent us Christmas presents. His son took over the business and Joe suddenly disappeared. No further details were offered.

*Thanks for all the laughs, Joe. I hope you're enjoying a glorious new "throne room" from wherever you are seated right now, my friend.*

# Ten

Construction has some wild cards. Some fun to play with, some, not so much. That's life. But who knew the parents of hockey-playing high schoolers could deal so much bullshit, too?

I'll never forget the German guy telling me, "Remember, when you are on stage, everyone in the audience is your critic." I learned that the hard way.

When I took over as the treasurer of my son's high school ice hockey team, they didn't have any structure, leadership, or a home rink. Ray and I got involved because our son, who was awesome at ice hockey, had just joined the team. Playing in mismatched shirts, they looked more like a street crew than a real team.

Club dues ran around $1,500 to cover ice time and other expenses. Some parents could afford to pay; for others, it was a genuine struggle. There needed to be another way to earn the right to play. So, I started doing fundraisers. The kids could earn participation credits shaking cans, doing trash pick up, bagging groceries and selling raffle tickets.

While they were shaking donation cans at the local grocery stores and delis, I was calling corporate offices pleading for raffle prizes. It was a ton of work to organize and host, but the events were profitable: $20,000 here, $40,000 there; $100,000 in all.

With matching socks, jerseys, a signed contract for their own home rink and a custom billboard donated by the AmVets, they looked official. They played better. It was an awesome transformation and wow, what a pay-off for all the hard work. After all was said and done, there was still plenty of money in the bank.

We only had one problem: little Johnny Merlino. He loved playing ice hockey, but four years of leukemia treatments left his bones brittle, and his parents broke. It was such a shame. His big dream was to get back out on the ice just one more time. There's only a small window of time for a kid to play high school hockey. And who knew if, or how long, Johnny would live. For now, his window on the world was from a bed at Children's Hospital.

I spoke to his parents. They were buried in medical bills and debt. So much was beyond their control, and my heart went out to them. I said, "Legally, you have to pay *something.* Can you pay ten dollars? Twenty dollars? Whatever it is, it's OK." They paid twenty bucks. Good enough.

Johnny was officially on the team. You'd have thought we handed him a winning lottery ticket the day he got his team jersey and a number. I got his equipment for him. Now all we needed was for him to play, even just once.

I went to the team meeting feeling pretty good about the turnaround for the club, and for Johnny. The kids learned that hard work pays off, and there are more ways than one to skin a cat. It was worth celebrating. Instead, I was ambushed at the door by an angry mob of parents chastising me about Johnny Merlino.

"Huh? What? What's the problem? Come again?!"

"You let someone play for $20?! Everyone else had to come up with the full amount, why not *him?!*" The mob spokesperson was yelling at me. *Don't yell at me.*

I could not believe they were pissed about helping a kid with cancer. Seriously??

I said, "You know what? I gave him *my* son's credit, how about that?"

Oh no, that wasn't enough. They started whispering behind my back. "Oh! She closed her company. Oh! She went bankrupt! She must be stealing money, then. We gotta get her out of there!" They repeated this to themselves so much they bought their own bullshit.

Stealing? I put in ten grand of my own money. WTF was it with these people??

The German guy said, "You're doing a great job. Don't worry about what they're all thinking because they're not doing shit anyway."

Giving them credit for being thinkers was a stretch.

It didn't matter. They built a case against me, and rallied to remove me from the club altogether. How that proved to be their best and brightest idea defies reason. Why didn't they rally to help a kid with cancer, instead? SMH

Trying to reason with, or understand people who are stuck on stupid, is an epic waste of time and energy. Delete the need to understand. It won't change what happened, anyway.

P.S. My doorbell rang at Christmas time. It was Johnny's parents, stopping by with a gift and great news: their son was fully recovered. And, he finally got to play in a game.

It was like our own personal 'Make-A-Wish' story with a good ending.

A decade later, the story lives on. Johnny still talks to my son about me; about how our fight for him to play changed his life. Now *that* is something worth repeating.

Just one year before we jumped in to help the hockey club, and for several years prior, RPM Construction was kicking ass. That was why the union came to 'persuade' us to rejoin their ranks, remember? Multiple projects kept us all hopping until "The Big Crash of '08."

Three of our general contractors filed bankruptcy in the same week. Shit rolls downhill. The money they owed us was supposed to go to the union. It didn't matter that the economy was *horrible*, the union still wanted their benefits payments. The letter they sent about the six figures we owed truly scared the hell out of me.

Frantic, I called my attorney. "Three G.C.'s just screwed me. The union is on our asses. I don't have the money. What the hell am I supposed to do?!"

"That isn't fair," he said. "You can't get left holding the bag." And yet, there I was, holding a big bag of shit.

"The union doesn't give a fuck. I promise you, they will take your house, Pat." He paused while I got up off the floor.

"They will take my *house??!* You mean, literally, like *literally* take my house?"

"If you owe the union, they will file to sell your house and take what you owe them, plain and simple. The only way out of this is to file chapter seven and eleven, business and personal bankruptcy, and hold the judgment. You gotta do what you gotta do, Pat. You have to protect your kids; your family. These people do not give a rat's ass about your predicament."

When swimming with sharks, get a bigger shark. I found the best bankruptcy attorney in New Jersey. None of this was my fault, but it became my responsibility...and personal living hell, let me tell you. Invoices, receipts, bank statements, 1099s, fuel logs, asset evaluations, depreciations, the cost of dog food and tampons. We had to bare our souls hoping a total stranger would see just how messed up things got in the span of a week, then pray he would grant us permission to dissolve life as we knew it.

I walked into that courtroom a sleep-deprived, stressed-out, nervous wreck. *St. Jude, don't fail me now.* I wished Ray were there. He was always so calm. When they called my case number I started to cry. Sob-sobs took over. *Oh, God, no.* The judge was like, "Are you OK??"

*Was I OK?? If only you knew, judge.* At the same time all of this was happening, I was also defending myself in that five million dollar wrongful death lawsuit. I felt terrible about that poor man, but the injustice of that judge, allowing them to come after me personally, was truly hard to fathom. Here I was, facing another judge for something I didn't do.

I said, "Judge, I was raised to pay my bills. I have an 810 credit score. They all screwed me in the same week. I just don't have the money." I told the truth. He granted us a mixed blessing, for sure. When you file for bankruptcy, they don't let you keep your assets. We had to give up all our trucks and cars. How were we supposed to make money without work trucks? I broke down watching my Escalade being taken away. It wasn't about the car. It's never about the stuff - it's about the impact. How was I going to keep the boys' life normal when I couldn't even drive them to school? As a mother, I felt like I failed them. As a business woman, I felt like such a loser.

THUD! Rock bottom hurts.

I thought about my mother's favorite expression, *"It could always be worse."* She was right. At least we got to keep the house.

A week or so later, totally out of the blue, my sister, Kathy, and her husband, Al, stopped by the house. They wanted to see the boys. I knew they were there to make sure I wasn't hanging out on any ledges. Kathy doted on our sons. They were the kids she never had. She said, "You can't have kids and no car, so let's go get you a car."

Naturally, I objected. "I don't need anybody's help." None of us bought the bravado. Kathy's credit enabled me to get a car. We split the payments and began rebuilding our lives behind the wheel of a Volkswagen CC.

Sometimes, God sends people to help you kick karma's ass. Let Him.

P.S. It'd been a couple years since the bankruptcy. I couldn't find some important documents, and called my attorney for help. Surely, he would have a record. I left him a message and opened the local paper to find this headline: *Legal Eagle Trades Trust for Time.* My lawyer had a record alright: an 'arrested and facing 17 years in federal prison' record. New Jersey's best bankruptcy lawyer was caught stealing money out of client trusts to pay for his house, boat and other status 'essentials,' like his son's hockey expenses! Thanks to the injustice of the justice system, the thief was only given a 10 month sentence.

Thank God that didn't happen to us. *See, Ma, it doesn't always end badly.*

But just in case, I told my husband before he died, "Babe, when you see God, ask Him to stop putting assholes in my life."

"I will when I get there, babe." He was laughing, but I wasn't. Enough already.

# Eleven

Meg was babysitting me when the hot iron accident happened. She'd turned away and I, the curious tyke, tried to iron like my big sister. I didn't realize how heavy that damn thing was, and it fell onto the back of my right hand, searing through all seven layers of skin, right down to the bone. The man in the white coat didn't give my parents much hope of recovery. "IF this heals right, the scar will become a problem as she gets bigger. It may, or may not, grow with her, we just don't know. It's going to be a rough recovery no matter what." He wasn't kidding.

I remember how my father would pull me onto his lap to have a look. Raising my tiny burned hand up to his lips, he would softly kiss the burn over and over again. "See, it is getting better. They said you wouldn't heal but you are healing. See? You are healing." I couldn't see any difference, but nodded 'yes' anyway. He looked beyond the moment, past the pain, and forecast a future without a withered hand.

"You are special, Patty. You weren't even supposed to be born, yet here you are! You were supposed to have mental challenges from a lack of oxygen, but you're the smartest of the seven. You are our miracle baby, and you will do great things in life. Don't ever forget how special you are." Planting kisses on my forehead was his way of saying, *OK, time's up, my leg is tired.*

Metaphorically speaking, when an iron scars your hand, 'spinning hay into gold' is an option. My father used the accident to instill positive beliefs, and it worked. An avid reader of "Prevention Magazine," Dad probably knew healing happens faster when you're positive about the outcome.

Scooting off his lap and marveling at my hand, I thought, *My daddy is magic! He can see the future! He says I'm a healer and my hand proves it. He says someday I'm going to do big things.* The future was always bright in Lefty's eyes.

# Twelve

Finding solid, reliable, responsible subcontractors is worth its weight in *platinum.* Most of them are up to no good, cutting corners, stealing time on the clock, or wasting thousands of dollars in materials. "Measure twice, cut once" never goes out of style, but how soon they forget.

It is no wonder I was red-faced from yelling: *I did the math.* When forty men take longer breaks, leave work early, and go to the john five times in a day to read the paper, or text their baby mama, I'm paying for it. Union benefit packages are pricey as hell. Let's see, 40 guys x average 1hr wasted per day is 2,400 minutes @ \$1.50/min = \$3,600 of *my* dime and time a *day.* Nobody thinks about that when they come back 15 minutes late from a 15 minute break. Like I said, *everybody's got their hand in my pocket one way or the other.* Someone is always on the take.

So, it came as no surprise when a new general contractor hired us to be subcontractors, but wrote up papers binding us to the responsibilities and insurances he was liable for. I knew something was wrong. *If it looks like a duck, and quacks like a duck, it's a fucking duck.*

I had to tell the client. I would want somebody to do that for me.

"Hello, is this Ingrid? I know you don't know me, but I was hired to build your new house and I have all your original paperwork."

Ingrid said, "Oh wow, that's so crazy. I never answer the phone for numbers I don't know, but something told me to take this call. Wassup?"

"My name is Pat, owner of Blue Diamond. My husband and I build steel frame commercial buildings. The G.C. who hired us as subcontractors for your house is up to something. I don't want anything from you except to tell you what I'm seeing after 25 years in the business. It's odd that he wants to list my company as the G.C.. It is a shifty move requiring us to hold the insurance and liabilities, not him, so we are declining the job."

Ingrid was paying for a metal framed prefab house. We were referred to this residential gig, and thought it was "meant to be" because, coincidentally, our business expansion plan included bringing metal framing into the residential industry in the northeast.

This move into residential housing was inspired by a huge fire that killed a lot of people in Ft. Lee, NJ. Metal is non-combustible, for starters. Their complex was made entirely out of wood. Wood is combustible. Duh. Metal doesn't mold, has no mildew, won't twist, warp or sag. Termites don't eat steel, either. However, Northeast Lumber lobbyists were squashing metal frame houses with a vengeance. They didn't give a damn about unnecessary deaths and destruction. Trees were money sticks to them.

Hurricane Sandy proved how much we needed to make the shift in building materials. I had all the trades on board to build high end, electrically-grounded, Certified Fortified metal homes. We were going to market the whole rebuild using impact glass with hurricane resistance. Ingrid's house was slated to be the first residence built as a way of demonstrating the vision and feasibility of our metal frame homes.

I said, "I'm not telling you to use him, or not use him. You go and figure out what he's up to. But as a good person, I would only feel comfortable handing your blueprints, drawings and original paperwork back to you, the owner of these construction documents. If he gets his hands on these he might hold them 'hostage' and limit your options moving forward."

Her new home was falling apart at the seams. Dead silence. She's a tough woman, too, but after waiting for so long to get her new house built, she was overwhelmed. "I'm going in blind! I have no idea what any of this stuff means. What do I do now? What *can* I do, Pat??"

For two years, Ingrid and her three children lived in subpar conditions until their home could finally be built. Her excitement turned into panic. The G.C. had $96,000 of her money and secretly intended to keep the majority of it. If she didn't ask the right questions to 'out' his shady business hustle, it would have gone really wrong, really fast.

What is it with "secrets" anyway?

My mind wandered off to the worst secret ever to strike our family. Earlier that same year, we discovered our oldest brother, Jimmy, kept his illness a secret.

"Jimmy" was too hard for me to say as a child. He was "Jige" to me and we shared special bonds: both left-handed, both beaten daily by nuns because of it, and the only ones, ironically, to get college degrees.

I guess he thought he was being smart not telling us he was so sick. By the time we heard about his secret, he was headed in for surgery.

"Only one person is allowed to visit him in pre-op," the nurse said. "Which one of you will that be?"

Brothers and sisters nervously glanced around at one another. Fortunately, God made Dalmatians and determined folks like me who run toward burning buildings. That may sound odd, but for some reason, I could always handle medical emergencies better than anyone else. I was dubbed the 'family fireman.' Breaking the awkward silence, I stepped forward with a loud, "I will."

The nurse led me down a beautiful corridor. The wall's colors were so comforting and warm. It almost felt spiritual, like a spiritual retreat center. I had no idea what I was walking into, so when she turned and said, "You're a brave woman to go sit beside a dying man," I was floored.

*A dying man.* We thought he had blocked bile ducts.

"Brave? He's my brother. Of course I'm going to be at his side. Where else would I be?" I bristled, trying to recover from the 5,000 volts she just tossed my way.

I took a deep breath, and tried like hell not to look confused about what was happening. "Hey, Jige!" I said, bursting into his room like it was a party.

"Hey, little sister, thanks for coming to see me."

"Of course! Where else am I gonna be today, huh?"

"You're supposed to be in Texas for Kevin's hockey game. What are you doing here?"

"Nah, that's not till next week, and maybe I'll skip it," I said.

"Promise me you'll go, Patty. He's a kid, please don't let him miss what he worked so hard for. I'll be fine."

After an hour or so of small talk, Jige was losing his voice. "Sis, I need water. I. Am. Sooo. *Thirsty*." He sounded like a character in "The Godfather." This was not acceptable. *When's the fucking surgeon coming in?!*

I rang for the nurse. "No. Pre-op patients are not allowed any liquids," she said.

His lips were visibly dried out by now. *What's it gonna take to give a dying man some water?*

"Then get me some ice chips! He needs water, can't you see that?!"

"No. Pre-op patients are not allowed any liquids."

"Then how about a popsicle, lady? Can we at least do that for him? Can't you see he's suffering? He needs a drink of something!" She didn't get the popsicle for me. *Fuck this.* I went and took it.

Dabbing his lips with one of those God-awful sponge 'popsicles,' I said, "Jige, don't you worry 'bout a thing. We will be right here when you wake up. And no matter what happens, no matter *what* it is, it's going to be fine." Dab. Dab. I smiled sweetly. He didn't need to be worried, he needed hope. "We are right here for you, Big Brother!"

With all my heart, I believe that if a dying person gets caught up in negative emotions their transition won't go so well. It's like they get caught, or stuck, hanging around, trying to let us know they are fine. I've even heard some say our mourning impedes their journey back to heaven…that we have to celebrate their life, not tether ourselves to their passing, or to past stuff we had between us.

Save the tears for later, hold their hand right now, and be optimistic, always. Miracles happen, right? People get better, right? I glanced at my right hand, remembering how Dad would kiss it and lightly draw a cross on it every day. *Please, St. Jude, make my brother better. He's such a young man, Lord. He's a good man. He has more life to live. We haven't spent much time together, God, so could you help us out down here and make this all go away?*

I still didn't know exactly what was wrong with Jimmy. In fact, "cancer" was not mentioned until the surgeon came out. He told us it was everywhere in Jige's abdomen; that there was nothing he could do to help. The news was dumbfounding. How did we not know about this? Why did he keep it a secret? Maybe we could have done something sooner? The 'what if' and hindsight theories didn't mean diddly-squat, really. It was already over for Jige.

I kept my promise to a dying man, and took my son to the Texas hockey play-offs. It was hard to focus when I was busy imploring the good Lord to rally for Jige. *Please God, please give us some more time together. We didn't know this was going to happen.* The phone rang. Finally, some news.

"Mrs. Miller? This is your brother's surgical ICU nurse."

"How is Jimmy? Is he getting better?"

"Ma'am, I called to see if you wanted to say goodbye one last time." I was the last person to speak to Jige because he never regained consciousness after the surgery. When she called, I went into overdrive phoning family to stand beside him before he passed-on. I hate that I wasn't beside him when he died. More guilt to carry. Perfect for a Catholic.

Then I realized, *putting water on his lips WAS my time with him*. With that thought, an eerie calm came over me. It was as if his soul was next to me in the car that night. Looking toward the sky, I found some stars to magically place his soul on.

My son and I flew home the next day to prepare for the funeral. If only he'd told us, we could have had more time together. Secretly, I cursed secrets.

"What *can* I do, Pat?" Ingrid's question snapped me back into the present. We'd only just buried my brother a few months before - I couldn't help being mad about people who kept secrets, for whatever reason.

"Well, what you can do is ask him for proof of insurance, for starters. That's his responsibility as the G.C.." I gave her several significant questions; things the 'regular Joe' wouldn't know to ask. If he didn't answer them properly, she had grounds to get her money back.

Ingrid called a few weeks later. "Pat, I gotta tell you that jerk failed the test." What's interesting is that she'd already been 'round and round' with that guy months before we got on the job. She said, "I told him back then that I work in law enforcement, and I *will* come after you. Just because I'm a woman doesn't mean you can take advantage of me. He tried to play me twice! If it weren't for you, Pat, I would have lost everything and been in trouble with the feds - it was *their* money on the line. I tell everybody that you're my Guardian Angel."

Was it coincidence, fate, karma or destiny that we were the ones on Ingrid's job? In the end, it doesn't matter; it's about playing the cards dealt, living with integrity, and refusing to allow hustlers to hustle. That's how the three of us worked together to kick karma's ass.

Ingrid said, "He was a fake businessman who popped-up on the scene. His con included meeting his wife, spending time with his kids…all to convince me he was a family man and that my family was in good hands. They were all in on the lie."

Secrets suck.

People will try to hustle, derail and degrade. They never learned to treat people with dignity, to respect them for their own sake, and to treat them ethically. That's *them.*

The only thing that can go wrong in your life is when *you* go against your own dignity and integrity. Think back to times when you said 'yes,' it should have been a 'no,' and *you knew it.* Trust yourself. Treat yourself with dignity. Treat others the same way. When you act with dignity, everyone wins. The bonus is you are helping without being a "fixer."

Just a quick note to those in power: you have the responsibility to act ethically and in accordance with your power. Doing otherwise is just bad karma, man.

P.S.: A few months later, Ingrid hired us directly to build her metal frame home. She'd just recovered from a two-timing cheater of a man and was done with being lied to. Finally, she and her kids had people they could count on, along with one helluva cool house to grow up in. We became her 'forward' in life. Years later, she wrote the foreword for this, my first book.

*See, Ma? Sometimes it ends well.*

# Thirteen

"Pat, I set off the smoke alarms!"

"Don't go crazy, Liz, you only need a puff!" I was trying to help her clear out negative energy by burning some sage.

"Ohhh, now ya tell me. I had a lot of clearing to do, ya know? But then my husband walked into a house full of smoke and created more negative stuff I gotta clear. When does it end?" We laughed our asses off. Her husband hadn't exactly been a cheerleader for her spiritual awakening processes.

Hey, at least she's trying to feel better. It takes a lot to come back from the night we had 13 years ago.

I'll never forget the jarring sound of police banging on my door, "Pat?! Pat Miller! It's the police. We need to talk to you, Mrs. Miller!"

Blue cop car lights lit up the front room.

*OMG, now what? If something happened to one of my boys, I'll lose my freaking mind!* I ran past the cops still standing at the front door. They could wait. I needed to see if my sons were OK, first.

It was early Sunday morning; both sons were accounted for. Whew. "Sorry to keep you waiting, guys, but I'm a mother first. Now, uh, what can I do for you? Why are you here, banging like that? What happened?!"

"I'm Sargeant O'Day. Mrs. Miller, there's been an accident. Your friend, Liz, said we should call you," he said. "Please come with us."

"Wait! What's wrong? What happened??! Is she OK?"

"We think it's best if you speak with her," he said.

*Oh God, why won't they tell me?*

Racing over there, I barely put the car in park and bolted for Liz's door. She was scream-crying on the floor, "Mmmmmmm. Mmmm.. Myyyy. My son! He's dead! He's *dead*, Pat!"

O.M.G. Phillip. Dead. No way.

I looked up at the police for answers. "She tried calling her husband, Dan, but he never picked up. She kept saying, 'Get Pat! Get Pat!' so we scrolled her contacts and found you. We didn't want to leave her here alone, ya know?" the officer explained.

She was able to get Phillip's father on the phone and sobbed the news to him. He said, "Why weren't you watching him? He was your responsibility! It's your fault he is dead!!" He yelled so loudly, for so long, that I grabbed the phone out of her hand, screamed at him to shut the fuck up, then hung up on him. As if she wasn't already hurting, he was blaming her for it? What an *asshole.*

Phillip tried to seek rehab but was turned down due to a lack of health insurance. What a shame.

All I could do was wrap my arms around her, there on the floor, while she shook both of us with deep sobs. I couldn't even begin to imagine how she felt.

So much changed that day. Phillip's death took the life out of Liz. Recovering from his passing prompted a pause in our friendship, as well. My son, Keith, and Phillip, used to hang out together a lot at the house. For Liz, just seeing my son brought her to tears. It was hard on all of us, and so, she stayed away for a very long time.

Phillip and Ray used to hang out and smoke in the garage. Ray loved to talk about his latest psychic reading, and since I didn't want to hear anything negative about the future, I was glad they had each other to talk to. Phillip would tell Ray, "I've never felt like I was going to live long." Little did I know Ray's response was, "I don't think I'm gonna be here that much longer, either, man." That was back in 2005, when he started pressuring me to learn his side of the business. Hmmm.

# Fourteen

"You're not gonna believe this," my friend said.

*Try me.*

"I went to an amateur astrology group to get a natal chart reading. I was hoping they could help me figure out if life was always gonna be such a battle."

"They say it's a general layout of your life, like a blueprint," I said.

"...and then some." She went on, "Patty, after staring at my chart for like 20 minutes, they picked their heads up from the chart and stared at me, all worried-looking. I didn't know what to think. Then the spokesperson said, 'We are new at this so we wanted to check-in, to see if we are on the right track. We think you were three years old when your parents got divorced. Are we close?'"

"They weren't close, they were exactly right. I mean, how do you get that kind of detail, Pat?"

Is it all already done? Was it on the chart that her father nearly suffocated her to death with a pillow when she was two, but they didn't want to ask *that* question to confirm their accuracy? Like, was it *all* there? If the divorce was dated, why not that, too? How predictable is life, anyway?

People immediately push back with, "Oh, but free will..." and my friend says, "It can look like you exercised free will to turn left instead of right, but maybe even that decision can be seen on the chart, right?"

It brings to question how much of life is predetermined, fated and unavoidable. It is one of those questions that doesn't come with a neat and tidy answer. Delete the need to understand, just play the cards in your hand, man.

# Fifteen

We were dealt a few bad hands at once. Well, for several years, really. After Jige passed, Mom and Dad got sick at the same time. My role was handling the medical stuff again. No surprise there. An endless stream of 'Oh nooo, *what* happened? I'll be right there!' added to the worry and stress that goes with aging parents. Running both of them to different hospitals, rehab, surgeries, ERs, and doctor visits, all while running the business, and being a mom, just about wore me out. Three of us kids worked out a schedule of care, alternating days and duties, for the better part of five years.

The hard part was watching my spunky mother go from having a heart attack, to being paralyzed and bedridden. She'd been running around her whole life, but now her bones couldn't support her ambition. What a horrible way to live out the rest of life. Our Slipper Ninja was slipping away, and we all knew it.

The early morning phone call came from my brother, Matty.

He and Kathy wouldn't be able to get there as fast as I could. My brother Michael agreed to meet me. Arriving 20 minutes beforehand, finding Mom in bed, with her mouth open, was a devastating experience.

Losing your mother is really tough. It's like cutting the string that connected you to childhood. In a single 'snap' a rush of memories flood your mind all at once, and experience the connection to them all at once, too. I spoke to her lifeless body as if she would answer me back, but her spirit was nowhere to be felt. Gone was the pillar of perseverance; the quiet woman who said little but when she did, everyone listened. In a way, my prayer that she be made more comfortable was answered. At least, that's what we hoped for as Michael and I stood over her body and prayed she would enter heaven like the Catholics promised.

It was the Monday after we buried Mom. Ray and I were back at work as if nothing had happened. And yet, it *had*: *my mom died.* Those are heavy words when they become your reality. A brick tossed through a plate glass window is more subtle in how it shatters your whole being.

Sitting in the office, trying to focus on business, wasn't much help, really. Sure, some of the stress was over. Yes, she had to be in a better place. Lord knows she earned a spot in heaven. Never was there a more dedicated mother, daughter, and wife.

Mom was the last one standing in her family. She watched her sister die of brain cancer at age 43; her brothers pass away in their 50s, then both parents, sick and aging, became her 'job' until they passed away, too. No wonder "life is for the living" became her one line motivational speech.

"It could always be worse," she would say. It's hard to imagine how, frankly. Mom raised seven kids without running water, in a drafty farmhouse with year-round cross-ventilation. We tried, but those cardboard patches just couldn't keep out winter wind and freezing temperatures. Summers were brutal with just one box fan between three bedrooms. I swore that when I grew up I would never be without air conditioning.

How Mom kept her sense of humor and perspective, that it could always be worse, and it could always be harder, was admirable. We all have it so easy by comparison.

The phone rang, ending my trip down memory lane. It was Ray.

He said, "I just got outta the john here at Ingrid's. Babe, I think I might be getting a urinary tract infection." He whispered, "I peed a little blood."

He mentioned feeling a slight 'burn' this morning before work. "Maybe it's just a urinary tract infection coming on,"

I said. "Go over to the walk-in clinic across the street, see what they say, Ray."

My thoughts ran to Dad and his struggles with urinary tract issues. The catheter he wore gave him nothing but pain over the last 10 years. What an awful way for an old man to live, having a tube stuck up his penis.

Thank God, Ray was healthy and fit. A blue collar worker *has* to stay in shape, or he can't work. No pun intended when I say that Ray built a reputation for invention. He was one of the few guys in New Jersey who could steel frame a 45-degree freestanding wall. Many architects recognized Ray for his talent, vision, creativity. *Nobody* could do what Ray Miller could do, free-forming metal into artwork, including a full size piano. Together, we built a multi-million dollar business thanks to his talent.

*"Ray Miller" 2014*

I thought of how Ray worked in the harsh New Jersey weather all those years, and how our sons, Keith and Kevin, do the same now. It's amazing how Ray's work ethic was passed down to them. It wasn't an easy path, but the reward, seeing how one of our buildings employed thousands of people where there was once an empty lot, felt great. Even so, our lives weren't exactly "fun."

For decades people asked, "Have you guys been to California?" Nope. "How about Las Vegas? Surely you've been to 'Vegas,' right?" Nope. For some reason, our 'vanilla' life blew people away. They figured we were partying it up and putting stamps in our passports with the best of 'em. Truth was, we hadn't been anywhere cool or fancy or fun. But that was all about to change. Very soon, these two little words, "change orders," would be great to hear instead of, *Oh God, not again.* Soon, "change order" would be *us* changing cabins on the Greek Island cruise. I could smell the salt air already.

Ray showed no signs of improvement over the next few days. I called Ingrid. We were close. You get that way when you build someone's house. I said, "Did you give my husband a UTI?!" I'm not sure who laughed louder. I have a weird way of letting people know what's going on in my life, I know. "Ingrid, we gotta take Ray to the doctor 'cuz something's not right."

On Monday, Ray was eating breakfast with me, taking his coffee out to the job site as usual. On Thursday, his urine could have passed for a cup of Hawaiian Punch. It was all blood. No shit. More like, *Oh shit. What's wrong with my husband?* He was going to need more than antibiotics this time.

One sonogram later and we were smacked in the face with the answer: a big tumor in Ray's bladder. The bladder is a reservoir for urine. When it gets full, you get the urge. When it's full of blood, you get help, *fast*. No wonder it hurt him to pee.

A week later, the tumor was removed in a procedure called a TURBT. The biopsy report returned on November 11, 2014. Ray was diagnosed with "highly, *highly* aggressive" bladder cancer. Yeah, that's how the doctor put it: "highly *highly* aggressive."

Ray didn't have any symptoms, but, like a cavity you didn't know you had until it hurt, everything seemed fine. Pain is the last signal that something has been wrong for a long time. Anyday, life can turn on a dime.

"Fucking cancer got me," he said, tossing out his cigarettes. It was prophetic, really, to watch him crush a silver box of Marlboro Ultra lights and have it trigger this sinking feeling in my body. Our plans circled around the bowl like his discarded cigarette box; a slow-motion fade-to-black like the end of a scary movie.

Everything went sideways that day. We just weren't sure for how long, is all. Highly, highly aggressive *anything* isn't a good assessment. Were they playing it down, or making a case for additional treatments? Was it that bad, really? I didn't know shit about shit at that point.

Hitting the internet, I discovered a key answer: if the *"highly aggressive"* cancer broke through the bladder's muscular wall, cancer would spread through the bloodstream. You would think that immediately removing his jacked-up bladder would be the first order of business, right? Yeah, that's what we thought, too.

Nothing too good for my husband, we got the best guy available: a world-renowned bladder cancer specialist. "Bladder cancer is largely curable. Not to worry. You'll see," he said.

What we saw, instead, was a protocol requiring Ray to have chemotherapy treatments for the next 90 days, *then* bladder removal surgery. If the whole-body chemo didn't kill Ray first, *maybe* it would attack cancer that *may* have already seeped into his bloodstream, *if* it had at all. That was a lot of *'maybes'* and *"what if's"* for such an aggressive cancer. Why not remove the problem in December, *then* do chemo to catch the 'maybes'? That made sense to me.

What I thought didn't matter. I was just footing the bill and trusting strangers with my husband's life. If he made it, would he rather live with an 'outie bag,' an internal Indiana pouch sewn to the abdominal wall, or an internal neobladder made out of his intestines? Regardless of our choice, we had to bow down and kiss the rings of their protocols. They might as well have said, *Our way or the highway, Ma'am.*

What should we do? Which way to go? I was up against the wall at a dark time in my life. And this, the million-dollar question: how could I *not* agree to do whatever it took to get Ray better? What price would you put on your husband's life? I couldn't live with myself if he died and I hadn't tried everything in my power to save him. I couldn't imagine the future, saying something like, *Oh yeah, Ray passed, but I saved a few hundred thousand bucks by going cheap, so I'm set.* Believe me, some people would do it that way, and for those reasons. We decided to go with the neobladder surgery.

'Turned out there was quite a bit they neglected to tell us upfront. Maybe they thought it best we didn't know the true aftermath of this type of surgery? How might they have worded "it will be like what a nuclear bomb does to the environment" and still get our money? *Brace for impact,* but keep it a secret. That's what it felt like.

The neobladder surgery involved removing his bladder, cutting a large section of intestines, shaping and sewing intestines into a pouch, then sewing that pouch to his urinary tract. Ray was on the table for 18 hours. I guess their seamstress was slow. Then again, intestines are lubricated; it must have been some trick just catching a needle and thread through them.

Ray came home with a catheter in his penis and a bag attached to his leg. That was so urine wouldn't interfere with healing the neobladder. But everytime he tried to pee, the catheter was clogged from mucus made by the lubricated intestines. He would do the saline flushes, but sometimes, the clog was so bad I had to help tug all the mucus out. As ugly, painful and difficult as all this was, Ray *never* complained. He groaned with pain, but he never complained.

Ten days after being released from the hospital, the results came in: "All the margins are clear," they said. That meant 'no evidence of cancer coming through the bladder wall.' Oh, thank God. Because if it did go through, it would flood his abdominal cavity, hit his bloodstream and spread. *Well, that wasn't going to be our story,* I thought. He was cleared. *Thank you, St. Jude, patron saint of hopeless cases.* We were filled with hope, at last.

Ninety-days more days pass, and guess what? *Happy 28th Anniversary, by the way, the cancer came back.* It was late May, six months after they first announced "this is a *highly* aggressive stage three." Chemo hadn't worked.

It is well-known that surgery stimulates cancer cells to metastasize. It is hard not to think, *If only they'd removed the bladder sooner than later, none of this would be happening*. But it was happening, and so, Ray was subjected to intense radiation treatments.

Every three months I would hold my breath and pray, *St. Jude, help us stay in the clear*. But no, more testing, more dissecting, then *Uh, the cancer came back.. We found another spot*. More radiation treatments. And waiting. And testing. And biopsies.

I remember sitting out in the hallway while they took another cell sample. Ray was screaming so loud, for so long, I jumped to my feet, ready to barge in and scream STOP IT! myself.

A nurse stopped me at the surgical room door.

"Why didn't you tell me you were going to torture him?!?"

She said, "Are you sitting out there in the hallway? Oh, you shouldn't be there, Mrs. Miller. You're not supposed to hear that."

"Hear what?! Ohhh, you mean his screams? You mean how you didn't sedate him before plunging an 18-inch needle into his backside?! You mean *that* part?!"

The truly barbaric exploration of his psoas muscle, the major muscle which allows you to get in and out of bed, went from bad to worse: Ray's sciatic nerve was inundated with cancer.

As if to waive the proverbial white flag of surrender, the oncologist said, "Let me refer you to my brother in New York. He's doing a bladder cancer drug trial at NYU."

*Oh, OK. Now that we have seen how waiting three months to operate, knowing it was "highly aggressive bladder cancer," was a bad idea; now that you've made money on chemotherapy that did nothing for him; now that you have profited from radiating, cutting, stitching, poking and prodding the crap out of my husband's body…now you happen to have a brother doing a bladder cancer drug trial one state away?* How convenient.

Oncologists are one of the few types of doctors who can prescribe a treatment from which they both directly profit, and administer, in their office. It went like this: "*Ray, you need to get this $15,000 shot. It forces your bone marrow to expel white cells. It's painful as hell and your whole body will ache from it. Now just move on down the hall to Room C and we'll get you going.*" So, yeah, that happened.

# Sixteen

The cancer trial was at Langone Hospital on 34th Street in New York. Ray's health insurance went up to $26,000 for the additional state's coverage.

We were handed a three-page script and required to follow it to the letter, or risk being kicked-out of the trial. Insurance paid for the doctor, thankfully. Although the big pharma company paid for the drug itself, the required number of scans, blood draws, biopsies, radiation, hospital stays, doctor visits, surgeries and pain medications were on me. Cash only.

I hadn't worked in over a year and we were bleeding money. Friends, family and "The Lending Tree" saved the day with their high interest personal loan. Ray needed to have a house to come home to, right? Bills didn't wait to see if my husband would get well again. In other words, life goes on while shit hits the fan.

My young nephew started a GoFundMe campaign for Uncle Ray. What a sweetheart. He said, "Aunt Tishy, you have so much on your plate, but here you are, baking me a cake and making sure I have a birthday present?!" His Christmas Eve birthday meant he got sorta 'ripped off' for birthday gifts each year. It was the least I could for him. No matter what's going on, birthdays are special.

Maintaining a sense of normalcy was damn near impossible. I did my best to be Mom, nurse, wife, dog walker, cook, and family fireman. Life as usual if you're trying to anchor a ship in raging seas.

I never needed anybody's help. To even be in that position, when retiring was our plan, was a big pill to swallow. That strangers would donate to our cause was truly humbling. The flipside was realizing that some of our rich relatives, with their millions and all, couldn't give two red cents, literally. I guess it shouldn't have been a surprise. Ray's mother never acknowledged her grandsons, either. It would have been a cold day in hell when I had to ask her for help. But, that it was never offered to us, was the real rub.

Borrowing money from family was something my mother would never do. Her side of the family could have helped, but Mom learned it came with 'interest' as well. Their hateful drunken tirades and snide remarks weren't worth the lifeline tossed in turbulent waters. *You don't have to eat shit just because you're going through shit.*

Fortunately, my immediate family chipped-in when, and how, they could. Ray made me promise to pay back every cent for every single loan, gift and grocery item. "I don't care if it's ten bucks, you pay it back. Don't owe anybody anything, Pat. I am going to send you lots of work from heaven," he said. *Thanks, babe, but God-only knows how I will manage to do your job, too.*

I just smiled and patted his hand. This wasn't about me. He was the one dying. My job was to make him as comfortable as humanly possible.

Ray felt so bad for getting cancer. "Pat, I am so sorry. I am so sorry I got cancer. I am so sorry I ruined your life." He cried so hard it broke both our hearts.

No one should feel bad that they are dying.

"Don't you worry about me, Ray. I'm a smart woman, and it's just fucking money. I can make more money, babe. You gave me a good life, and I'm going to do whatever it takes to save yours." Nevermind that I was losing my best friend.

Sitting there, day-after-day in that hospital room, facing his mortality with the Beastie Boys playing in the background, nurses checking his vitals, eating sandwiches together, was about as surreal as it gets. I sang Bob Marley's "Three Little Birds" to him all the time. *Every little thing is gonna be all right.* It was as much for him, as it was for me.

Of course I would survive. What was I gonna do, lay down and die right along with him? Of course I would make it. I just didn't know how. A dying man didn't need to hear a word of that, so I smiled, and sang.

I used to tell him, "Ray, it's going to be a lot easier for you to die without me, than it is for me to live without you. Where you are going is beautiful..." I trailed-off. He knew this was living hell.

"I will be there waiting for you, Patty."

I'd kiss him good-night, cover him up tight, and turn out the light. "See you in the morning, babe."

If traffic was really good, it was door-to-door, New Jersey to New York, in an hour. I tried to arrive in time to catch 8am doctor rounds. If traffic was slow, gridlock meant more time to worry, yell at God, and cry. Judging by the stares, I must have looked like a crazy person to the other drivers. *Look, honey, that poor woman is losing it right over there. Look! Look! Wow, she must be having a really bad day.*

*More like years of bad days...*

When those elevator doors opened to Ray's floor, I held my breath and prayed. The nurses meant well, but they had no idea how to care for someone with a neobladder. *Welcome to the School of Saline, Boys & Girls.* What were these people being taught in school again, please?

So, OK, fine, it was on me to train Ray's nurses to do more than dole out drugs. If I didn't do it, they wouldn't know any better, and Ray would suffer. Then whose fault would it be? You can't count on the men in white coats to know any better; I learned that firsthand, too.

Before Ray got sick, my brother-in-law, Al, became seriously, and mysteriously, ill. For 58 long days, that sweet man laid in a hospital bed suffering while doctors scratched their asses. They were getting *stupid rich* being stupid. Sorry, not sorry. What a racket. Furious and frustrated, Al became my project. In four days' time, I figured out what was wrong with him; HIT they called it. Then I told the doctors *exactly* what Al needed: high doses of vitamin K and steroids.

My dad used to tell me I was practicing without a license. He was so adorable. "Doctor Patty" they called me. If someone wanted a recommendation they knew who to call. *Hello? Yes? Oh, you need a surgeon? What kind? Oh yeah, I can refer you to a good one. He's expensive, but you want him to get it right, right? I think he got Bs and Cs in college. Not bad. Here's his number: (212) RICH-GUY.*

The mental anguish, physical output, ever-changing schedules, appointments, emergencies at all hours of the night…all of this went on for years before Ray was ever sick. There wasn't a 'sanity specialist' who could help, or she would have been on speed-dial, trust me.

Meanwhile, my father wasn't doing so hot. There were times I was in the E/R with Ray, and Kathy was in a different hospital with Dad. Lefty knew his time was coming. Often, (not always), when a person knows their time is near, they soften, say nice things and sometimes, for the first time ever, say "I love you." What I didn't expect was an apology.

"I'm so sorry for the way I treated you kids," he said. "It wasn't right and I'm so sorry."

"It's OK, Dad, you didn't know any different." I didn't want him to get stuck in this world because he felt bad about the past. "You know Dad, ya gotta get a license to drive, but there's no manual for being a parent," I said. I hoped he would let himself off the hook as much as I had.

"I forgive you, Dad." Letting go of the past is important. Forgiveness is how we move forward. Still, it isn't easy to forget the times he was apologizing for: that man could throw a mean left hook around the corner of a wall and never miss. In fact, I still have sensitive spots where his closed-fist punches connected with my head. None of us will ever forget peeking in the window at night to see if it was safe to go back in the house, then tip-toeing up that creaky staircase, praying that we didn't wake up Lefty. No doubt, my brothers have sensitive spots where the belt caught 'em one too many times, as well. When Dad was on the warpath, it was every kid for themselves. Mom was stuck in the middle, running interference, or just plain running. Sometimes, that meant she hid in the woods with us.

"That's how it was back, then, Dad. You know, everybody had that going on, it wasn't just us." Back in the 1960s and 70s, everyone we knew had at least one alcoholic parent. Once he sobered up, a new person showed up. My sons think I'm lying when I tell them how he used to be. *There's no way you're talking about the same person, Ma.* Their version of grandpa is a gentle, soft-spoken, funny guy that made everyone feel good. And eat. You couldn't visit without eating something.

"Sit down! You hungry?" When company came, it was salami and provolone time. Don't forget the black olives. He loved serving them in bowls.

His real joy was when I stopped by for dinner. "So tell me what's new? What are you building?!" He could hardly contain his excitement.

"Well, Dad, *you* know how these assholes are, right?" Just about every story started that way. Like Mom said, "It's always somethin' with you."

He would practically stop chewing so he didn't miss a single word. My daily life was play-by-play sports action to him. Mom would just roll her eyes. Then, no matter how the story went, he was like, "Atta girl, Patty! That's *my* daughter! You get 'em girl!"

"You're the president of my fan club, Dad." He would turn his head away, but I saw that smile.

"Patty, you're one-of-a-kind," he always said.

It's like I had two fathers: the one growing up, and the one he grew up to become. See? People can change if they want to. Look at that man's sparkle. To think he was 80 years old when this was taken:

*The author with James "Lefty" Ferrano*

After our mother passed, Dad was never the same. There aren't any quick fixes for a broken heart. He knew it was time to go and be with Mom. And so, he did.

I cried for my dad, and my heart broke for Ray. All he wanted was to say 'thank you,' or 'good bye,' or, *Hey, Lefty, I'll be seeing you soon, dude*, but cancer wouldn't let him.

Holes in hip bones don't lie: Ray's body was riddled with cancer. The tumor returned, too. So much for the bladder cancer drug trial.

We were so glad to be back home in New Jersey. The quiet countryside brought peace and relief from a year's worth of insane stress. Even our little dog was happy to see us home more often. Until now, Al was driving in 2-3 times a day just to walk her for us. Kevin took over in the evenings. The next day, it was lather, rinse, repeat.

On this particular night, I was in the kitchen making us some dinner. Out of the blue, Ray let out a blood curdling scream. The 9-1-1 operator could barely hear me over Ray's shrieking.

He'd been having difficulty flushing his neobladder. Nothing was coming out, and the additional pressure was causing extreme pain. Paramedics arrived to escort him back to his second home, the local community hospital. "Protocol," they said.

I never felt so angry and helpless all at once. I knew what he needed, but it didn't matter. Precious time wasted on protocol. Kinda like the protocol to use chemo for 90 days instead of removing the source right away, huh?

"Doc," I said, "I've been seeing pieces of food and cucumber seeds - stuff I can recognize - in his bag. It's been like this for a month now. It's getting worse. He is clogged up all the time. And, now he is in excruciating pain."

"Oh, just another UTI; it comes with the territory," he said, then sent us back home. That lasted like five minutes before Ray was writhing in pain. That was no urinary tract infection, damnit.

Scooping Ray up in my arms, I carried him to the car. After laying him across the backseat of the Buick LaCrosse, I drove it like I stole it. Screeching to a stop in front of the E/R at Robert Wood, I blew past the reception window. Ray could be heard screaming through two panes of glass. It was *bad*.

"HELP ME! My husband! Somebody, HELP ME!"

"Ma'am? Ma'am! Uhm, excuuuuuse me, but you will have to wait your turn. Have a seat, please."

*Have a seat? Yeah, no, not so much, but thanks.*

They barely got him into a room when he let out the mother of all screams. Internal pressure was built up so high that when he screamed, it forced the blockage. The dam burst. Feces came out of places I didn't know it could. There was so much back-up urine Ray was a human Pepsi bottle - the two-liter size. No wonder he hurt like hell.

From breast bone to pelvic bone, they fileted him open like a fish. The million-dollar neobladder had exploded, filling his abdominal cavity with feces. All my efforts to keep him clean, and avoid infection prior to this moment is probably what saved his life.

"I can't believe he's still alive," the surgeon said. "I've never seen anything like it. His organs have fused together from all the radiation, Mrs. Miller. His tubes are actually reversed. This is the worst thing I've ever seen in my life." *Oh, that phrase again.*

"OK. So, he's alive?"

"Yes, we cleaned out his entire abdominal cavity. It required *gallons and gallons* of saline just to ward off septic shock. The wound can't be closed, yet. It would only fester."

"So, is he just like, *open*?"

"Pretty much. We had to do a very loose rubber retention suture so air can get in there and healing can happen. The neobladder was moved aside. Removing it would take hours more in surgery. His body couldn't take that, so we gave him an ileostomy, which sits higher in the body."

OMG, poor Ray. His midsection looked like Frankenstein's neck. To clean his stomach, I had to work in between the red tubing they used to protect his skin from the stitches themselves. The Saline Queen strikes again.

Fun fact: Whether you eat or not, the body is constantly processing urine and waste. For Ray to stay well, he needed me to flush out his bag, saline-wash his stomach area and try to keep the pus in check. That routine had to be done every two hours, and it went on for four months.

There was not a lot of beauty sleep for either of us. If you looked at me, you'd have thought karma was kicking my ass. The truth is, it was. Until the day came where I could find value or a lesson in all this, life felt like a fist fight for no good reason.

I had to wonder what I did; was this the only theme for the rest of my life? I looked to the heavens and asked, "Are you sure I signed up for this shit?" Should I have run like Forrest when our wedding cake fell? Was the Universe trying to tell me something before I said 'I do'? I heard lots of people say, 'Naw, they'll never make it.' Isn't it nice to have love and support like that? We made it 36 years, 29 years married until death did we part. Even then, we left it as, *I'll see you later, man.*

Was Ray my karma? Was I, his? Did we have an agreement to swap roles as caregivers? Or was it less tidy, and I owed him big time for a past life fuck-up? It could be. Everything happens for a reason.

I don't regret for a second that I ignored the falling cake-omen, kissed my new husband, and got on with the business of building a life together, *come what may,* and no matter what the haters had to say.

"I can't believe you're still with me," Ray said. "Any other woman would have said 'Fuck you, man. I'm not pushing you in a wheelchair and I sure as hell ain't changing no ileostomy bag.'"

"I meant it when we took our vows, Ray. I'm faithful as the day is long, and I gave you my word at the altar."

No one expects "in sickness and in health" to mean someday, you might be wiping random spurts of pus and feces off your face. When that happened, as it so often did, he would start crying, "I'm so sorry! I didn't mean it!"

"I know, babe. You can't help what your body is doing. It's OK." While he slept, I cleaned body fluids off the furniture. When I tell you it was terrible, it was *terrible terrible.*

In and out of hospitals, Ray became somewhat of a freak show. Doctors from all over the tri-state area came in to stare at the spectacle of sutures and fused guts. We could have sold tickets. How weird would it be to have total strangers examining your body as if it, *you,* were a cadaver?

Let's not forget he was still dealing with cancer eating away at his sciatic nerve. Even the dilaudid and fentanyl patches (I snuck those in), hardly affected him. As one doctor put it, "I can't believe he is sitting up and talking like we are at lunch or something. Most people would be knocked-out, but he's as straight as an arrow. I've never seen anything like it." We heard that phrase a bit too often.

"Yeah, that's my husband, the medical wonder, huh?"

"Well, you certainly are, Mrs. Miller. You've saved his life a few times already. How did you know what to do and when to do it?" he said.

"Research. Intuition. I don't know, a little of both, I guess. Maybe I was a nurse in a past life, Doc. Maybe it's because I've had to take care of my brother, mother and father and the 'training' was all for this, eh?"

Reciting the sign I saw everyday at Robert Wood Johnson's Cancer Ward, "You never know how strong you are, until being strong is your only option," seemed to satisfy his curiosity.

# *Seventeen*

I must have put a hundred thousand miles in that year alone. The 'tour' of hospitals made a star on the map. It didn't matter if Ray was five, or sixty-five minutes away, my brother Michael visited often. They were very close. There is something to be said for being in the company of someone who loves you at your worst possible time in life. It is helpful and healing on a whole other level.

Al was at his side almost every day, too. Bagel or donut and coffee. Guy time. They were true friends. After being in the hospital so long himself, Al knew how much it mattered to have company at your side. He was often at my side when it was time for Ray to check out of 'Hotel Hell.'

One day, the three of us stopped at the pharmacy on the way home from the hospital. You would think you could leave two grown men alone in a car for a minute, but no, Ray whipped out a THC pen and started puffing on it the minute my door closed. By the time I got back with his prescriptions, the car was *loaded* with smoke. Coughing in the back, Al, (the veteran detective), was freaking out.

"Ray! I can't get tested with this shit in my system!" Poor Al. He was worried about his job as a security guard.

Ray was off his rocker, laughing hysterically. "Don't worry, man, it can't hurt you."

An hour later, we got a phone call from Al. "Ray. I think I got the munchies."

You gotta laugh. Al, in his 70s, catching a contact high. Nobody saw that coming.

P.S. As "Doctor Patty," I read cures for cancer, weed and cancer, essiac tea...I had my husband drinking roots, even. You name it, we tried it. Nothing worked. A beer after chemo? So what. "I don't care," Ray said. I'm so glad that he did. He was skinny and loved candy. Let a dying man have whatever the hell he wants.

Al was with me the morning after Ray went back to Robert Wood hospital. The night before, Ray sneezed. That was all it took: one sneeze and his intestines flew out of his abdomen. Ray caught them in his hands. My son, Kevin, was amazingly calm for a 21 year old watching all of this happen. As Ray held them tightly, I covered them with gauze and saline, then called for an ambulance.

More drama with paramedics and protocols. I said, "His *intestines came out* in my living room! He needs to go to Robert Wood. That's the trauma center you idiots!" It didn't matter.

"What in the hell are you doing here?!" The community hospital E/R doc was yelling at me. "This is *trauma.* We don't do this kind of trauma here!"

"I told them that. It didn't matter, obviously." I was beside myself.

"Well, get him back in an ambulance and take him to Robert Wood!"

*Yeah, no kidding.*

So there we were after the worst night of my life (so far.) Ray's burnt bladder and intestines were mixing and fusing together thanks to the additional radiation treatments. It was all on display through the red tubing criss-crossing his abdomen. A parade of strangers in white coats waltzed-in to get a peek at the medical freak show. What was this, a class or something? Four random people stood there, ready to take notes. *Who the fuck are these people??*

We waited to hear what the doctors had to say. Last night was pretty bad, and we all knew it wouldn't be great news, but maybe…I mean, we had hope. God-knows we were a praying bunch, asking for a miracle healing. That's when the wrecking ball, his oncologist, came in.

"Ray, there is nothing more I can do for you. Get your affairs in order." He announced it like game day results, with zero emotion. All eyes turned to stare at Ray's face when the pronouncement was made; it was as if they wanted to record the expression of a man being given a death sentence. *What would he do? How would he look? What would he say? Would his Frankenstein stitches split if he cried? What will his wife do? Will she cry, too?*

Can you imagine being the one laying there half dead, vulnerable, sick as a dog, and hopped up on so many damn pills you would have been arrested for public intoxication in any other setting, and *that* bomb is laid in your lap by the man responsible for frying your insides??

But wait, no, we're not done here: the added bonus was being *eternally fucked*. "Organs don't work when they fuse together," he said.

No shit, Sherlock. I couldn't believe he said that in front of Ray. I must have looked dumbfounded, so he repeated himself, adding a shoulder shrug, "Nothing more we can do."

It was all I could do to not grab that creep by his throat and throttle him right there. Instead, I grabbed him by the elbow and dragged him into the hallway for a wee chat: "YOU ARE SOOO FUCKING FIRED IT ISN'T FUNNY. How DARE you speak to my husband like that after all we have been through thanks to YOU? You don't make announcements like that in front of a dying man, let alone with random nurses and techs gawking at him. How about some privacy you callous son of a bitch?! What the FUCK is wrong with you?? Get your notes, your gear, your people, and get the hell outta here *YOU FUCKING ASSHOLE!!!*"

That whole incident *still* makes my blood boil. I don't wish bad things on people, but I'd be lying if I didn't say this: I hope karma kicks his ass, *twice*.

Newsflash, A-hole: it doesn't cost more to treat people like human beings.

His brother, the one doing the drug trial at Langone, had great bedside manner. A hand on your shoulder, or taking extra time to talk, he was always so kind. Somehow, he got the genes for decency while his brother got the douchebag genes.

Got a dick for a doc? Doctors can learn bedside manners and why it makes people get better, faster - if they want that sort of thing. "Love, Medicine & Miracles," by Dr.

Bernie Siegel, is a mega-best-selling book. Send the book anonymously and include a short note: "Dear Dick, Just read it. Learn how to comfort patients and their people. Or get out of the business."

Not all doctors are oblivious. "Mrs. Miller, I worry about you. Doctors don't typically see this much action. Veterans coming back from the front lines haven't dealt with as much guts and gore as you. You're living a Vietnam life, you just got the bombshell from hell, yet, you don't seem to be rattled by any of it," one doctor said.

"Would you be happy if I collapsed right here, or would you prefer that I run around the hospital crying?? I have two kids to take care of; I can't fall apart. What good would that do?? They need me, and so does that man *dying* on the other side of that door. I can't melt down in front of him, bawling over his body. He's the one dying, not me!"

I think he meant well, but at the same time, it felt like he was "professionally observing" me, looking for signs of insanity or something. It's simple: I just put the bad stuff in the back of my mental filing cabinet, kept my head down and sprinted for *years*.

Nobody saw me cry, but especially Ray. And I intended to keep it that way.

# Eighteen

That third round of radiation for cancer on his psoas muscles and sciatic nerve was just too much for Ray's beaten body to bear any longer. I was so grateful the pain pump I'd been asking for all along was finally approved. However, within a matter of days, thanks to the pump, his brain went loopy. He thought he could walk after that, so we had to hold him down. Confused, extremely high on opioids and a danger to himself, I faced the biggest decision, yet. It was hard to know the right thing to do. Making him "comfortable" during his last days on earth also meant silencing his voice. It meant he went unconscious. What if he wanted to say something to our sons, but couldn't open his eyes to blink out the message? To this day, I wonder what he might have said if he'd been able to.

Before he was totally knocked-out, the woman who gave birth to him came for a visit. A social worker was present; probably a good idea. Ray apologized for any hurt or inconvenience he may have caused, then told her "I forgive you for what you did to me as a child and I love you,

Mom." In one swift motion, she threw him an icy glare, did a little "pat-pat" on his hands, and walked out. A choreographer couldn't have crafted a more orchestrated exit. Poor Ray. I felt so bad for him. You can know someone's gonna stick it to you, and hope they don't, but don't count on it.

Nudging me to the hallway with a nod, the social worker said, "I have seen a lot of dysfunctional families, Mrs. Miller, but never, in my life, have I witnessed a mother being so cold to her dying son."

"Ray poured his heart out to her. She didn't even deserve it. Now he can pass on without any guilty feelings to hold him back. No unfinished business. That's all that matters: that he goes in peace."

"I have to wonder," he said, "how peaceful I would feel with that much rejection from 'Mom.'"

Using heavy sedatives would relieve Ray of thinking that way, too.

My cell phone rang while Ray 'slept.' I answered it out in the hallway wondering, *Who could this be? Everyone who knows me knows I'm sitting here waiting for my husband to die.* Ray was days from dying.

Three months earlier, once we knew for certain that he was terminal, Ray pushed me back to work. We hadn't swung a hammer in nearly two years. We won the bid and I started the job, knowing my brother Michael and a few other talented guys were on site. It was the perfect set-up for slowly getting back in the swing of things...and generating some income, finally.

I answered the call, "Hello? This is Pat Miller."

"Hey, Pat, how you doin'? It's Carl, the Super on your job."

"Yeah, I'm OK, I guess. It's been kinda rough. What's up?" Superintendents don't call for no reason.

"Well, uh, the bottom line, Pat, is the owners need you to be on the job site next Friday or the contract goes to somebody else."

"Is there a problem? I mean, I was out there a few weeks ago. What's the deal, Carl?"

"Well, you know how corporate is, right? They got rules. You gotta follow them. The owners want to see the owner, or the contract gets pulled."

You would have thought he was telling me to move my car or it would be towed. I said, "Carl, you know I sit by Ray's side every single day. You know he doesn't have long to live. Why are you telling me, out of the blue, that I need to make a personal appearance all of a sudden??"

I waited for an ounce of compassion - or a crack in his story. It sounded fishy to me. I'd seen it before: guys will resell a contract and pocket the difference.

"Pat, you know it isn't me, it's corporate. They are gettin' sketchy about no boss around, so you gotta make an appearance by next Friday. I don't know what else to say. It is what it is."

"You know Ray is terminal, right?"

"Doesn't matter how sick he is, Pat. In fact, the client doesn't give a fuck that your husband has cancer. This is business."

I wanted to slug him through the phone. *Filter! Filter! Find your filter!*

What choice did I have? I knew Al would come sit with Ray next Friday, no problem. Hopefully, that wouldn't be the day God called Ray home.

Sigh. "OK, fine. I'll be there next Friday. Thanks, man." I'm not sure what I was thanking him for, or that he even heard it. That gave me 8 more days to sit with Ray. OK. I could live with that.

Damn. What the hell was their problem, anyway? The job was going fine.

"Yeah, yeah, I'll be there." *Jesus, buddy, what the fuck?*

Ray didn't technically hear a word, but he knew. I have no other way to put this: *he knew.* The very next day, exactly two years from his diagnosis date, November 11th, Ray Miller died.

Damn. Those words are so final. We'd been through hell and back together. Ray was in heaven now and I was still trudging through hell.

I told the coroner, "Take out the Frankenstein stitches." I didn't want my husband buried with those still in him. Cremation, funeral, and finally, the wake dinner.

My phone rang while I was passing pasta to Michael. "Are you gonna be here on Friday, or not?" It was Carl.

"Can I call you back? We just buried Ray this morning. I'm kinda busy, man. We are having a repass dinner with my family right now. "

"I don't give a damn about your dinner or your dead husband, Pat. Are you going to be here tomorrow, or not?!"

"Yes. I said I would, and I will."

After all I went through, wondering what the hell I must have done in a past life to have such crappy karma, there's *Carl*, driving a fucking screwdriver into my heart, clearly enjoying himself.

The world was a cold-hearted bitch and he, its poster child.

# Nineteen

It was D-Day.

Swinging my legs over the bed, head in hands, I cried my eyes out. How the hell did I get *here?*

My business partner, best friend, high school sweetheart and husband, was gone. Everything fell on my shoulders as a mother and business owner. My life savings were gone and I owed $250,000 to all sorts of people.

I headed for the shower. *Maybe the water will drown out the sounds of me crying?* I didn't want Kevin to wonder if his mother was about to have a meltdown. The last thing I wanted was for either of my sons to think Mom needed taking care of, now that Dad was gone. I was not going to become their problem. Not today, not tomorrow, not ever.

Whoa. The face in the mirror was ragged as hell. It was mine. I couldn't believe it. Roots showing, no haircut for far too long, broken nails and polish that took the last train to Albuquerque months ago. Tore-up from the floor up.

The final curtain had been drawn for Ray. As I pulled the shower curtain aside, it felt like this was my curtain call. The spotlight was on me…and it really hurt my eyes.

Ray was the face, the frontman; the one who played golf with clients and drank with the boys. When perks came along, they landed in his hands. He conducted the show, I followed his lead. I was fine playing in the orchestra. He was the talented visionary who planned and built epic monuments in metal. The dynamic duo, that's what me and Ray were. I leaned on him, he leaned on me. We were an incredible team. Sure we had fights. *Fuck you.* Yeah, fuck you, too. *What do you want for dinner, babe?* Whatever you make is always great, honey. *I love you.* I love you more, babe.

We balanced each other in ways no one saw or understood. Him dying was like losing the leg off a 3-legged stool. What the hell was I gonna do? What choice did I have? Nobody from Publisher's Clearing House was ringing my bell saying, "Congratulations, Pat Miller! We are going to pay all your bills for you."

The hot water felt good on my sore body. Through the steam, I looked up. Surely he was looking down at me. I said, "Ray! Can you hear me? You know I gotta go do this, Ray. You know I want to pull the covers over my head and

The men are vicious in a whole other way. Like vultures, they circle overhead, seeking to exploit weakness. As one of the few women in the business, let alone "The Lady Boss," I became all-too-familiar with little boys who have sold their souls for greenbacks, traded compassion for crassness, and deemed themselves mightier than thou.

I did not want to be judged on sorrow. And please, don't pity me. I knew it was my turn to carry the cross. The last thing I needed, or the company could bear, was someone a-hole saying, *Oh, look…there's poor Pat Miller over there crying in the corner because her husband died.*

Just because I didn't shed a tear in front of them didn't mean I was a cold-hearted bitch. It *had* to be done this way. I was swimming with sharks that swarmed at the first sign of blood. I am not recommending my way, I'm just telling you what I had to do to transition from Ray's passing to slinging steel again.

Work wasn't the only transition I had to make, of course. Coming home to an empty house only echoed the aloneness I felt. It used to be that when Ray walked in the door, dinner was waiting for him after a long day. Kisses on the cheek and "Tell me about your day." These were decades-old routines. When I walked in the door, the house was dark, nobody was making me dinner, doing the dishes, or laundering the dirt-caked clothes dropped at the back door. The paperwork I typically did while Ray was on site still needed to be done. 'Burning the midnight oil,' and no one to confer with, became the loneliest job in the world.

The only plus to being alone was that no one heard me wailing my heart out all night. Ten hours on the job, then eight hours at night, wrapped around my dog and a box of tissues. That one routine was both a saving grace and a wretched grind: Cry to sleep. Get up. Put your boots on. GO!

For six months, I drove my guys really hard. We achieved the impossible, and everyone knew it. Completing a half million square feet of fit-out work in six months, to those who know, is *ridiculous.* To celebrate, the company owner invited me out for a drink.

"You ran this job like a pro, Pat! We are so grateful for all you guys did in such a short period of time."

"Well, it's not like I had a choice, man." He looked confused, so I continued. "The Super told me you were going to pull my contract if I didn't show up in person by a certain date, even if I just buried my husband the day before."

He goes, "Are you freaking kidding me?? We would never do that."

He continued, "You're fucking telling me that you came to this job the day after your husband was buried? I'm finding out *today* that you're a *widow and you came to our job for six months with a smile on your face*?!"

"Yeah, Carl said you were corporate and needed to see the company owner's face or lose the contract, plain and simple."

"We're a family company. We would never do that!"

*Who knew?*

Glancing at him over the rim of my glass, I raised an eyebrow, took a celebratory sip, and let him stew on the news for a minute. Carl. What a prize. Everything he told me about the company and their 'mandates' had been a lie. He messed with my life and tried to crush my business for a buck.

Instead of getting mad, I burst out laughing. So seldom do we get to personally hand someone their karma on a silver platter. A Friskies Whitefish Buffet silver platter, that is. You see, Carl is the same guy mentioned in the introduction. You know, the one who got caught on the job stroking off to cat porn?

He was the one I tormented with stuffed cats and cans of Friskies Buffet all over the job site. Is it coincidence or karma, that he was the one that had it coming? *Damn the luck, eh, Carl?* Meouch.

It wasn't long before Carl and crew were let go. The job was done and the owner took me under his wing with a half million dollars in maintenance contracts; a much-appreciated leg-up. I was back in the game.

However, unwilling to play the real game, 'Be My Side Piece,' possibly cost me millions in future work. The reason? "Pat, your prices are too high." *Uh huh. So are yours, man.*

# Twenty

"Hey, Jaime. How you doin'? The usual." I slid onto the barstool beside a 30-something woman. "How you doin'? I'm Pat. Hey, Jaime, did you catch that?!"

She said, "'Looks like you could really use that drink. Pardon me, but what just happened?"

My make-up was a bit 'off' and so was my vibe. Sizing her up real quick, I dove right in. There's something luxurious in pouring your heart out to a new person. They don't have any judgments and are usually just looking to talk.

"Well, I just met this man at a restaurant bar in Florida. He was full of life, happy about buying this-and-that, happy with his single life, just happy-happy about everything, you know? We hit it off right away. I loved making his chubby face get all red. Some of my jokes are funny, some are just dirty."

She laughed. My wine arrived. We were off to a good start.

"So," I said, "we're having a good old time, like old friends just sitting there on a park bench, laughing. And I sez to him, 'Paulie, what happened? Why are you sad? I see it in your eyes.'

"He goes, 'Patty. You saw dat? People who know me my whole life don't say nuttin' like that.'

"We just looked at each other, then he said, 'My son died a year ago. Overdose.'"

The young woman bit her lip. We both felt bad for the jolly fella.

I continued, "I know what it's like to put on a face. I also know money, sex and food can't fill the void. Broken hearts see broken hearts, Paulie."

I paused, took a sip, and waited for her reaction. There was an elderly gentleman on her right. I could tell they were together, sort of. I wasn't there to interfere with their date, or whatever it was they were doing; just needed a drink. Seeing Paulie's broken heart reminded me of my own.

"Hey, uhm, the name's Barbara," she said. "That's Duke." She smiled, he waived. "Take that purse off your shoulder, girl. Settle in and tell me more."

I put my purse on a hook, set my keys on the bar. "I know what broken-hearted looks like, Barb. I just lost my husband, Ray, a couple of years ago. In a few short years ago, I was over a million in the hole, too. I know what it's like to have every plan crushed like a pack of cigarettes. I know how hard it is when you're trying to come up, and haters wanna keep you down with stupid shit they say like, "There is no way that widow can recover on her own. She needed that man.' *Fucking ignorant people!*"

"No wonder you saw so much heartbreak in Paulie's eyes," she said.

"Yeah. Losses like that take time to heal and are really hard to hide. I had to do it for work, just to get by. Here's the funny part of a really shitty time: there was this Super on my job, Carl, a cat-porn loving creep who lied his ass off trying to steal my contract while Ray was in hospice. Like, how low can you go, buddy?"

"Cat porn?! Are you serious?" Barb was eyeing me with suspicion.

"Stay with me. Here's the thing: we all knew he was jerking-off to cat porn on the job, so I set-up pranks all over the jobsite for months. Embarrassed the fuck out of him, too. It was a riot. Ironically, when I was doing that, I had no clue he'd lied to me from the jump. He messed with our lives, lied about the client, and forced me to show up the day after Ray's funeral. I really didn't know he was lying about all sorts of shit until the job was over. I guess you could say karma got dished out to him with a flat of Friskies Buffet."

She laughed again. Humor, when going through hell, helps us all.

"Oh, if it'd been me I woulda sued," she said. "I mean, cat porn?? Oye. What's with men anyway?"

"Yeah, I get it. But a woman in a man's world can't be a crybaby or 'a lawsuit waiting to happen.' I was in a bad spot, and, of all things, that jerk-off actually helped me."

"I find that hard to believe. What good can come from a scumbag like that?" she said.

"What he did was shoddy and shady as hell, but he forced my hand. I hadn't worked in two years, had massive debt, kids that depended on me, and a mortgage to pay. I was exhausted. Staying in bed for a few years sounded like the best idea ever; just not an option. There was a lot of ground to cover and nobody to help me, you know?"

She was like, "Uhm, no, I don't actually know at all. I've had a husband since forever. I can't imagine what that was like for you. I'm separated, headed for divorce." She lowered her voice, "I'm scared to be alone. I don't know what I'm gonna do."

Duke patted her on the arm as if to reassure she wouldn't be alone; not tonight, anyway. "I gotta whiz," he said, sliding off the barstool. *Oh, it wasn't affection, it was a notification.* "If you don't see me in 10 minutes, come look for me." The pace he walked, it was going to take him 10 minutes just to reach the john. *What is he, like, 90 or something? Don't worry, I didn't say that.*

I said, "He's like, 75, huh?"

She nodded, then switched the subject by poking my key fob. "Ohh, boy I had that wrong. I woulda sworn that was your husband's caaar." Her rough Brooklyn accent reminded me of 'Pesci Joe.' I had to laugh.

"Nope, it's my car. I promised my dying husband that I would pay everybody back, to the penny, and then get the car of my dreams."

Her mouth fell open. "Wait! You got a Lambo?? Are you shittin' me?! You *bought yourself* a Lamborghini?"

Her voice got real shrill at the end. Other people glanced our way. Awkward. I hate it when rich people tell you how rich they are. The ones with real money don't talk about it. *Look away, people. Nothing to see here. Shut up, Barbara.*

I shrugged. "I love driving fast. It's my therapy without the therapist's bill."

Right about now is the point when people let me know who they really are: deep or shallow. Dudes love a fast car, and love a blonde who loves fast cars even more.

What people don't seem to get is I'm not the douchebag buying a flashy car to make up for SDS, (Small Dick Syndrome.) It isn't a status symbol, it's a toy. And what they will probably never know is that I'm the same girl driving my truck as I am a Lambo. Nothing changes. I just happen to like taking corners at 75 mph. You can't do that in a Prius.

Barbara looked skeptical. Like most people, they assume the worst and go from there no matter what you say. It wasn't flash, it was 'fast' I wanted.

Meanwhile, "The Duke" was pissing, or had gone missing, not sure. She didn't seem too concerned about him, so I continued. "Don't be afraid that you'll be alone, Barb. Endings are hard, but sometimes, life makes decisions for you and it turns out better than you ever thought it could." Throwing my head toward the Duke's empty stool I said, "Whatever you decide to do next is what determines your destiny. You don't have to compromise."

"Oh, you mean The Duke? It's just dinna."

"Yeah, sure. Dinner. I get it. You guys keep each other company over soft food and alcohol. That's real nice." I laughed to take the edge off a hard truth. I'd met more than a few women in the middle of a divorce "just having dinner" with dinosaurs. I couldn't help wondering whether Duke preferred chocolate or caramel sauce, since she was dessert.

"No, you don't understaaaand."

Ohh, that shrill voice. Then she said, a bit too loudly, "I mean, come on...saggy balls?!" and winked, like I oughta know how it is at my age.

*No. Just, NO.* I might be starting over in my mid 50s, but there was no way in hell I was gonna need an old dude to "buy me dinna" once a week.

"Sooo, that's your caaar, huh? You got it by yourself? How? How'd you do it? Like, for real, I never met a woman like you before, Pat."

Her attitude went from 'yah, right' to genuine interest. *Maybe my story would inspire her?* I said, "The secret to success is a four-letter word, Barbara: w-o-r-k."

So many haters in my world are haters because I have what they want. The problem isn't me, it's that they want the goods without doing the work. Then, when they get money they get stupid, blowing paychecks at the bar, or leasing Ferraris they can't afford.

"Listen, Barb, it ain't about the money, but to most people, it is. That ain't me. You can't let your job, your car or the size of your house define who you are. Haters make ignorant decisions about shit they don't know shit about. That's been the hardest part for me, really: seeing how many haters there are in the world. You would think that a woman coming up strong, on her own, would be applauded or somethin' but it isn't…it's a reason to call her a bitch and run her down."

"YOU built your company back all by yourself, though? That's hard to believe," she said. I've seen people struggle with the idea. If a man did it, it's expected. If a woman does it, it's suspicious.

"You sound like them with their *'Impossible!'* That's what they said behind my back. *Just watch,* is what I said."

"Yeah, but you wuz by yourself after all those years?"

"I wasn't alone. Ray was around me. I could feel him. And he would leave me signs."

I was out washing the car shortly after Ray passed away. Two doves landed on my garage. I'm like, *Is there a wedding or something? Doves don't normally visit the New Jersey countryside.* Might have been angels, I dunno. Two years after that, feathers started showing up *in* the house. I have so many now that I could stuff a pillow.

"How did you know it was him? I mean, birds are birds, right? It coulda been a coincidence," she said.

"Yeah, I thought that, at first. Then the penny-plus-a-dime stuff started happening. I would find eleven cents in the weirdest places, like, under the center of my bed. How the hell does a dime and a penny end up underneath a king size bed, right?"

My mother was born on the 11th; Ray died on the 11th, and was diagnosed on the 11th. Maybe I was making meaning out of eleven. I've since learned it's called a "master number" and has spiritual importance. Back then, I just wanted to know which one of them was leaving a penny and a dime together all the time. Weird.

"Riiiiight," she said. "That's pretty cool, but it doesn't pay the bills, girlfriend."

Just then, "The Duke" shuffled back onto his stool. "What are you two hens squawking about?"

Barbara came to life. I didn't know she had that much energy in her. "Duke, this lady is amazing! She lost her husband and made a million bucks, *by herself,* in the couple of years since he passed, Duke. You gotta listen to 'dis!"

Her enthusiasm reminded me of Anthony Farinaccio, a nice Irish boy. Just kidding. I think the Lord puts people together for a reason; if nothing else, to share a story and a laugh. Anthony is one of those people.

We met because of his car detail business. The first time he did my car it took 12 hours. Not really. He was done in a snap, did a great job, and pulled up a chair to chat about business. "You can only do so many cars in a day, Ant," I told him. "Look for something that doesn't have a glass ceiling." I wasn't trying to fix, just help. It's so rewarding to talk shop with an open mind.

"Barb, it isn't what happens to you, it's how you get back up. Don't quit. Go with what you know and grow from there. I was inspired by Anthony, too, ya know. Such a young kid with so much heart, eager to see the positive when life knocks you down; he's going places. He has the right mindset," I said.

The Duke was curious. "So, what is it you do, young lady?" I appreciated the little wink, but could do without the tongue flicking gesture. *Saggy balls. Eww.*

Smiling, I said, "I try to keep men's hands outta my pockets, how about you Duke?"

"I get more action with my kisser than my pisser." Another wink.

*I'm not touching that line with a 10 foot pole.*

I said, "I run crews of men. My company builds large commercial buildings all over 'Jersey. I couldn't have gotten this far if it weren't for my husband, though," I said

"Wait, I thought you said your husband passed away?! Oh, I just knew you were kidding all along." She turned to The Duke. "She said her husband passed on and she done this by herself."

"Yeah, he is, Barbara. But he never left." I pulled out my cell phone. "Look at this big feather I found on the deck the other day. Once he got diagnosed with cancer, he built that gigantic deck all by himself. That's where I found this huge feather, sitting on the doormat outside the kitchen."

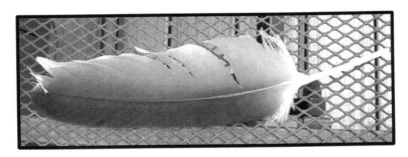

The Duke tried to look interested in what I was saying but his eyes kept drifting to my heels. When you're that old, cheap thrills are about as good as it gets.

I went on, "I'm telling you, I'm not alone. Ray is around. I talk to him in his urn all the time."

Old Duke looked up from my legs, shocked. Things just got weird for him.

If I didn't call on Ray I don't know where I would be. I was 'stuck like Chuck' trying to make the soffit go around the plumbing pipes and duct work. I would sit there for hours but could not figure it out. After two days of trying, I was a nervous wreck. I needed to get that job. No matter what I did, it didn't work out. Shuffling through 120 pages of blueprints, with a quarter of the floor plan on each one, was so bad it would have made a nun swear.

So, I said, "Ray! I've had enough coffee breaks and walks, man. I need to see through your eyes, babe. Show me what I'm missing." For some strange reason, I went and put his urn on the table and backed it up by wearing a pair of his eyeglasses. I was like, *Come on, Ray, I really need your help.*

It worked. Instantly, face palming and all, I was like, "OMG! That's IT! That's the only way this would work! OMG, you are so right! Thank you, babe!!!" Converting that nine-story office building into 117 apartments was how I rebuilt my company in a year.

I'm so grateful to the Developers and G.C.s who trusted me to build their structures. Being off for two years made the climb back very interesting, but my contacts made it easier. Even so, with every single job, I have to prove myself worthy of it. Fortunately, referrals are happy to say, "Hell, yeah, that woman knows what she's doing." My partner, Mo, says that one of the best things about working with me is having vetted professionals who show up, do the work, and leave quality behind. Knowing who does what really well saves time and dime, not to mention grief, change orders and nicks in your reputation.

I tell my realtor, Sean, "Listen up, Mr. Rodriguez. The magic bullet in business is being a connector. You got that in spades, young man." He is all of 22 years old and, last I checked, went from $0 to over half a million dollars, in spite of covid, in just three years, by connecting with others.

I turned to Barbara. "A smart man learns from his mistakes, but a wise man learns from the mistakes of others. The positive side, the one I like better, is that we can get help calling on higher wisdom for guidance, like with prayer. That's how I bounced back: I called on Ray, prayed and worked my ass off. If I can do it solo, anyone can."

She stood to go. "Pat, here's my number. Duke, I'm sorrrrry, but I have a headache. I gotta go."

As Barb walked out, The Duke leaned closer to me. "My kisser is better than my pisser!"

"Yeah, that's what I heard, Duke." I threw him my crooked smile and got up to leave.

He quickly puckered up. I patted his hand and said, "As tempting as that is, I'm gonna have to pass tonight. I already ate dinner."

# Twenty-One

People cross our paths for a reason. Cat-loving Carl's crap turned out to be the best thing that could have happened, believe it or not. Sure, he lied like a rug. In the end, his antics forced me out of bed. I might have taken a day or twelve off after the funeral, otherwise. As a business owner, that could have turned out pretty bad for my future.

As a mother, I couldn't just collapse; I had my sons in mind. I am so proud to have raised men. They inherited Ray's work ethic, too. If I 'lost it,' how would that impact them *for the rest of their lives*? The Miller legacy of taking care of one's parents was going to be broken by me, come hell or high water. I am so grateful to have children that given my life purpose, and me, the strength to carry on.

As a widow, I owed it to my husband to rebuild our company. We worked too hard for me to return to 'employee status' as a corporate accountant somewhere. Ray's death was not in vain because I became the woman I was supposed to be. No more subservient, shadow-dwelling 'voice of the company' for me…in fact, getting out in the field with my hot pink hard hat and big mouth is working. Who knew? Men I've only spoken to for five years come up and say, "I know that voice. You must be Pat Miller, right? Gosh it's nice to finally meetcha!" The other day, a phone call followed a meeting I attended. The G.C. said, "Pat, I have to hire you. You were all they talked about after you left. Apparently you know your shit." *Yeah, I do, I've done this many times over the years, you tend to learn from repetition.*

As a woman with integrity, I had to keep my word. Ray's dying wishes were "Live your life! Find someone to talk to about business; someone who gets you! Travel! Do the things we planned to do!" He wanted me to move on. And so, I did. I met a construction professional, (perfect), who has restored my trust in men, (cue shock face.) *That* is a big statement. Mark is one of those steady guys you can count on to have your back. What a blessing! How good is it to know that not all men are trying to pick a widow's pockets?

As I close this chapter of the book, I want you to know that personal transformation isn't scary, but the circumstances behind it might be. And that's OK. It is all new territory, so it's normal to be nervous. But don't let that stop you. Ask for guidance. Look for signs. Follow the nudges. Whatever you are called to do, is for you.

Not too long ago, the calling for me was exploring "readers," like Ray did. Rick the Prick put me into a tailspin, I'm not gonna lie. I felt so rejected and confused, *Why God? After all I've been through already, why?* That 'breaking open' moment nudged me to dive deeper for answers. That led to a YouTube channel; it just felt right, like I was supposed to find it. The hosts, Frankie and Desiree, are supportive, enlightening and intuitive women. Their insights have affirmed, and confirmed, that I'm not crazy; yes he was a karmic liability, and hooray, I'm clear. Yes, there *is* more to life than what we currently know it to be. And yes, there *is* meaning in the feathers, three crows and gray fox peering at me through the fence. Feathers, pennies and dimes…and now, dreams…Ray has literally come through to push me to write this book…the one you now hold in your hands. There *is* a reason for everything, and everything happens for a reason.

Personal growth reminds me of a houseplant: it can only get as big as its pot. All the events you read have grown me right out of that pot I was planted in, thankfully. Already, there is so much more to share with you! I can hardly wait to write Book Two.

The story doesn't end here, but the book does. However, if you would like to get bonus stories which didn't make the cut, and some key 'Saving Your Sanity' tips for a tough time, please visit www.KickingKarmasAss.com

P.S. Recently, I went to bed crying, asking Ray if I was on the right path. In the morning, inside the sheets, I found a small feather, a dime and a penny at my feet. Eleven cents. Go figure.

Made in the USA
Middletown, DE
04 September 2024

59732099R00110